62.

D1436679

Dunfermline Abbey.—*Frontispiece.*

THE FRINGES OF FIFE

NEW AND ENLARGED EDITION

BY

JOHN GEDDIE
Author of "The Fringes of Edinburgh," etc.

Illustrated by Arthur Wall and
Louis Weirter, R.B.A.

LONDON : 38 Soho Square, W.1
W. & R. CHAMBERS, LIMITED
EDINBURGH : 339 High Street

Printed in Great Britain.
W. & R. CHAMBERS, LTD., LONDON and EDINBURGH.

TO

GEORGE A. WATERS

of the 'Scotsman'

MY GOOD COLLEAGUE

DURING A QUARTER

OF A CENTURY

FOREWORD

' I 'll to Fife.'—*Macbeth*.

MUCH has happened since, in light mood and in light marching order, these walks along the sea-margin of Fife were first taken, some three-and-thirty years ago. The coasts of 'the Kingdom' present a surface hardened and compacted by time and weather —a kind of chequer-board of the ancient and the modern—of the work of nature and of man; and it yields slowly to the hand of change. But here also old pieces have fallen out of the pattern and have been replaced by new pieces. Fife is not in all respects the Fife it was when, more than three decades ago, and with the towers of St Andrews beckoning us forward, we turned our backs upon it with a promise, implied if not expressed, and until now unfulfilled, to return and complete what had been begun.

In the interval, the ways and methods of loco-motion have been revolutionised, and with them men's ideas and practice concerning travel and its objects. Pedestrianism is far on the way to go out of fashion. In 1894 the 'push-bike' was a compara-tively new invention; it was not even known by the name; it had ceased to be a velocipede, but was still a bicycle. Now, along with the foot-passenger, it is being pushed off the road by the more hustling and speedy, but mechanical, motor-bike, and still more by the ubiquitous motor-car and motor-bus; and with these there have been twisted into the main threads of human life and experience the telephone, the gramophone, the 'wireless,' and, most portentous of all man's recent inventions, the aeroplane.

The world has changed, and with it the Fringe of Fife; although, fortunately, there are still long stretches of it in which you can walk and imagine that you are in the end of the nineteenth, or for that matter, of the sixteenth, century.

The wrinkles and the pencillings of art and utility which the last three or four decades have marked on the forefront of Fife are too many and ubiquitous for cataloguing in detail. Some scars, however, are more than skin-deep; they penetrate, not indeed to the 'soul of things Fifish,' but to the quick, and will take time to heal. For a few samples:

The railway has drawn its score between the old causeys and biggings of Culross and the sea; and it has similarly treated Low Valleyfield and its adjuncts —a convenience doubtless, but, at many points, a sad break in historical continuity and in pictorial harmony of effect. At Crombie Point and Ironmill Bay there are grievances, for the wayfarer, of an opposite kind. For while great buildings have risen on the shore and a pier stretches halfway across the Firth towards Boness, the Admiralty have flung an iron arm bristling with spikes around this part of the shore of Fife, shielding it from the foot and eye of the unauthorised intruder.

It is a relic of the Great War; but nothing, in elaboration and extent, to that which meets us a little way east of the old churchyard of Rosyth. A 'Naval Base,' with its immense and costly appurtenances of docks, wharves, derricks, and storehouses, occupies all the space to Inverkeithing, and stretches far out into the Firth. It has set its signal-poles and flagstaffs on the adjoining hills; planted a new town between the coast and Dunfermline, and appropriated Rosyth Castle as an Officers' Club. The future fate of the former headquarters of the High Seas Fleet, whence it sallied forth to keep the enemy within his ports, or to drive him back, and finally to bring into these guarded waters the surrendered navy of Germany, still hangs suspended. Never will it be forgotten that to Fife men were committed the supreme charge of the defence of the realm, by land and by sea, at the most critical hour of its history—to Earl Haig, as Generalissimo of its Armies, and to Admiral Lord Wester Wemyss, as First Sea Lord.

Meanwhile Rosyth is promised preservation, as a base of reserve destroyers. By its annexation Dunfermline has been brought down to the sea. The Palace, the Abbey and the other antiquities of that Seat of Kings, the burial place of Canmore and the Bruce, along with its unequalled modern amenities, that to do them justice would require a volume to themselves, have become incorporated in the sea-fringe of Fife.

Inverkeithing, except for its core, has been transformed by the same agencies; an aerodrome has settled down on the lands of Donibristle; St Fillan's Church, at Aberdour, has been roofed and restored; Inchcolm. its rocks still cumbered by naval works, but its ancient Abbey made more intelligible by excavation, has become a regular tourist resort, to which a steamer plies from South Queensferry; aluminium works have taken possession of the precincts of Old Burntisland and of the inlet resorted to by the Roman galleys; and Rossend Castle is turned into a boarding-house and tea-rooms. Change has been scarcely less busy farther east, about Kinghorn and Kirkcaldy, at Ravensheugh and in Dysart; the old shore path by Barncraig and Macduff's Castle is almost deserted, the roof of the Glass Cave has fallen in, and the adventurous little golf-links, set among rocks and caverns, is abandoned to the sea-maws. Methil, become one of the most 'populous places' in Fife, has annexed Buckhaven and Innerleven, and has connected itself with Kirkcaldy and other neighbours with busy tram-lines and motor-routes.

Changes have come also to Leven and Lundin and Largo; to Elie and Earlsferry; to St Monans and Pittenweem; to the Ansters and Cellardyke; even to Crail and to the East Neuk. Some are to be regretted; more, perhaps, are in the form of improvement. They are signs of growing popular favour as watering-places and golf resorts, more seldom of growing industries. They but mark the way of the world, and need not be enumerated. The borders of Fife are not the less worth passing survey, or intensive study, in these days when 'the way of the world' seems to be tending more to the monotonous and the commonplace. In essentials Fife preserves its individuality; and what was written of this in the Foreword of the edition of 1894 may stand:

The days were of the shortest when we set out on our pilgrimage around the Fringes of Fife. Our purpose was to seek and seize, as opportunity offered, the soul as well as the form of things Fifish. Such a quest is best made under grey skies, and in a nipping and an eager air. 'Not in summer but in winter,' Andrew Lang tells us, 'is the time to see St Andrews'; and what is said of its chief shrine may be said of 'the Kingdom' at large. When cold weather and easterly *haar* resume their reign there is a flitting of the migrants that settle for a season on the shores of Forth and Tay. The golfer no longer haunts so persistently putting-green and bunker. The camp-stool of the artist is removed out of its place commanding some stretch of sand and sea, with the waves breaking white on rocky ledge or pierhead; the nook of some little fishing haven where the boats are hauled up or lean aslant at half-tide, or the *howff* under the lee of the whitewashed gable wall where wide-breeched, weather-beaten gossips sun themselves. The last of the bathers and holiday-makers have fled with the leaves. Alien types are weeded out. Fife is itself again.

Only when the land has been thus purged and cleansed—after you have faced the wind from the North Sea that plies, through the winter and spring, its untiring rasp on the edges of the headlands and shrills round the seaward projections and callosities of the ancient buildings down by the shore—can you trust yourself to read aright the quaint hieroglyphic, of Nature's handiwork and man's, that is written along the margin of the Fife coast. The little burghs huddling under the shelter of cape and high ground; the red-tiled, steep-ridged houses crowding together and turning their crow-stepped gables and forestairs to the street and their backs to the blast; the forlorn little graveyards on the brink of the salt water, each with its group of old tombstones and storm-stressed trees gathered about some fragment of ivied ruin; the Dutch-looking kirk spire and town-house steeple sturdily asserting themselves beside the new schoolhouse and literary institute; holy caves and wells, under a canopy of pit-smoke; dilapidated salt-pan, and malt-barn, and doocot standing cheek-by-jowl with present-day villa and factory stalk—all are seen to be native to the element and to the scene. They have that indurated, strongly marked individuality which belongs to Fife character as well as to Fife architecture. They are the expression of all the past weather and past history of the province. In the jargon of later science, they are reactions to the stimuli of their environment. Much of this the summer wayfarer misses.

Furthermore, it should be said that our survey of the hem of Fife was not carried out continuously. It was made by short descents, in scraps of leisure time. The reader may amuse himself, if he likes, by marking changes in weather, season, mood, and companionship, and employ his ingenuity in picking out the seams in a loosely-woven narrative. But he may rely on it that every step of the way was faithfully trodden. We clung to the coast line as closely as was consistent with the rights of private property. Never for long were we out of sight and sound of the sea. It may be said that this was but skimming Fife. The reply is that by such skimming one may gather the cream of the Kingdom. Its richest essence has condensed and become encrusted on its outer surface. The selvage, as King Jamie hinted, is worth the web. And this is said in full remembrance of Falkland and Dunfermline, of Cupar and Markinch, of Dura Den and Lindores Loch, of the slopes of the Ochils and the Lomonds.

CONTENTS

13

LIST OF ILLUSTRATIONS

THE FRINGES OF FIFE.

KINCARDINE TO TORRYBURN.

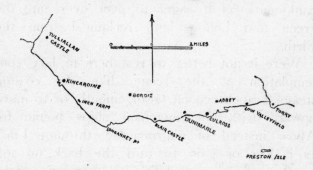

Fuimus.—Bruce Motto in Culross Church.

THE river-boat drops us at the pier of Kincardine-on-Forth, and holds on its way with the breeze and tide. But still we linger at the landing-place. It is not a scene to part from hastily. The pathway of the broad river, straight and burnished and tapering like a sword blade, stretches away towards the heart of the Highlands. Stirling Castle and the Abbey Craig rise above the carselands where the Forth winds its links of gold, and overlook the battlefields of the War of Independence.

Behind them, in dim outline, are Ben Lomond
and his neighbours—friendly giants of Rob
Roy's country that guard a land of enchantment. Nearer at hand are Dunmyat and Ben
Cleuch and other crests of the pastoral Ochils,
the purple shadows nestling in their folds and
haze, or smoke from the chimneys of the hill-
foot villages, trailing across their skirts. Beside
us, the brimming waters lean against the em-
bankments, as if eager to peer over into the
green and hollow land reclaimed from the
Firth.

Were it not better to rest here in lazy con-
templation of the scene, like the coaling
steamers anchored off Grangemouth, or to move
upward with the merchant ships bound for
Alloa, instead of pilgrimaging through Fife?
Is it loss or gain to turn the back on soft
western skies and hills, on vapoury peaks
melting into clouds, and set the face to the
keen sharp air and hard and bare bounding
lines of the North Sea?

Kincardine, when we have made our way
into it, does not afford large compensation.
Its streets come straggling up to the neighbourhood of the Cross, and stare vacantly at
each other. They are wide and clean enough,
and have some marks of eld, but they are
wanting in distinction as well as in cheerfulness.
The sap of life flows slowly through the old
barony burgh. It has seen better days. The

very houses are built upon the ashes of its
former prosperity—upon the ejected refuse of
its five-and-thirty salt-pans. Gone, too, is all
but the name of the potent spirit of Kilbagie
that inspired the mirth at Pousie Nancy's.

Many of the houses date from the latter part
of the eighteenth century. It was then that
Kincardine stirred itself up to great things in
the carrying trade. In its palmy days it would
have as many as nine vessels on the stocks
at one time. Its tonnage was more than half
that of the port of Leith. It had vessels trad-
ing to the West Indies; it sent whalers to the
Greenland Seas; a large share of the coasting
traffic was in its hands. But these days are
only a memory; and an air of deadly dullness has
settled down upon it. Yet the inhabitants had
enough of spirit left to resent their inclusion
by the Boundary Commissioners of 1889 within
the realm of Fife. 'Me a Fifer!' said the
young lady of the tobacconist's shop whom we
had incautiously complimented on the change.
'I'll never be a Fifer. I was born in Perthshire.' This prejudice is not unknown among
the neighbours of the Kingdom.

Behind the town is the handsome parish
church of Tulliallan, crowned by an ornamental
square tower. Farther back and higher up,
enclosed on three sides by the Tulliallan woods,
is the dismantled older church, with its surrounding churchyard. It is unroofed, but the

Dutch-looking spire, built in the Restoration period, still fronts toward the water. On the stones may be read many a sorrowful tale of the sea, of the time when Kincardine was peopled by shipmasters and mariners. The names are here, but the graves are scattered wide—'Died at Rio,' 'Drowned at Sea,' 'Buried at Moscow.' Deeper in the forest, also girt about by its little graveyard, are the fragments of the pre-Reformation church.

It would seem as if the population drew closer down to the shore as land was rescued from the river bed, and that the Church and the Dead had laggingly followed in the wake of the living. Old Tulliallan Castle, already a strong fortalice at the time of Edward I.'s invasion, had once stood on the margin of the Forth, as it now does almost on the western bounds of extended Fife. The moat, encompassing the strong grey walls screened by their little clump of wood, was filled from the river, now half a mile away across the level green fields. Its fine groined and vaulted hall, still in fair preservation, must have echoed in its time to much rude revelry. For its old masters, the Blackadders from the Merse, were a turbulent race, too ready with hand and tongue, and the good deeds of Robert Blackadder, Glasgow's first archbishop, is hardly a set-off to the account of their acts of sacrilege and murder.

For a mile the 'low road' to Culross does not begin to rise. The flat and fertile land, the high embankment damming back the river, the lines of poplars on the other shore, bring memories of Holland. A deserted roperie trails its way down to the roadside from the green slopes on the left, and beside it is the embattled gable of a ruined jail—industry and authority in decay. Near by is the Inch farm ; and as we look through the porch a tug with a brig in tow comes sliding along the top of the embankment, as if drawn by an invisible string, and disappears in the direction of Longannet Point.

This apparition we follow eastwards, until the road begins to rise and twist round clumps of firwood and to skirt the parks of Sands. On the hill above there is a glimpse of the tower of Bordie, behind which, in the moorland, is the Standard Stone marking the scene of Sweno's defeat by the army of the 'gentle Duncan.' Along the shore is rough pasture and plantations with brushwood overgrowing the mounds of rubbish ejected from disused coal-pits and quarries. Wide was once the fame of the close-grained, marble-like sandstone of Longannet and Blair. The Register House in Edinburgh was built of it, and in the seventeenth century the Dutch are said to have sent hither for the stone used in the Town House of Amsterdam. Here and there the rock gleams through the wood in pretty bosky places, and great white ledges protrude from underneath the grass and trees upon the beach like giant ribs.

And now the high land pushes down to the coast. The slopes are covered with wood or terraced in gardens, and the road winds below. From behind the cliff appears, close down on the shore, a group of roofs and a quaint steeple, and beyond it a noble sweep of bay.

This is Culross, a nook of Fife difficult to get at, and still harder to get away from. Railways do not come within two miles of it ; no passengers by water land at its little pier. The wooded ridge sweeps round it so steeply and closely that the trees and hanging gardens look directly down upon the Sandhaven and the West Green. It is like a protecting arm thrown around the forlorn old royal burgh. Here it has tucked itself away and gone to sleep—a sleep of centuries ; and the world has forgotten that in its day it set afoot great enterprises, showed how coal could be mined under the sea bottom, taught salt-making and the virtues of coal-tar gas, and sold its girdles throughout the Land of Cakes.

It is a corner into which Time has amused himself by raking together a choice collection of his curiosities in architecture and in character. We do not enter, however, immediately, or from this side. Crowning the hill above the

little Episcopal Chapel of Saint Serf is a sheaf
of towers. It is Dunimarle, and occupies, it
is said, the spot where erst Macbeth swooped
on the nest of the Thane of Fife and slew all
his pretty chickens and their dam.

There is an invitation to climb up and look
around on one of the fairest sea-scapes in Fife,
or in Scotland. We may even enter the castle
and examine the museum of antiques and works
of art, the library, and the collection of pictures
left in trust under the will of the late Mrs
Erskine Sharpe. Everything is grandiose and
monumental—the white terraces, the avenues
of dark-plumed yew, the battlemented gateways,
the great iron gates. Along a sombre approach
of araucarias and wellingtonias we stroll, until
we strike a delightful cross-road wandering
away into woodland glades, and shortly come
upon the sequestered nook where the remains
of the Old Parish Church of Culross are
hidden.

A little farther and we reach the road coming
down from East Grange station,
past Blairhall, the cradle of the
Bruces, Earls of Elgin and Kincardine. The gothic tracery on the
gable wall of the 'Chapel Barn'—
now the West Lodge to the Abbey
House—announces the neighbour-
hood of the venerable Abbey Church ; and at
the turn of the brae we come suddenly upon

Coat of Arms,
Blairhall.

the massive and pinnacled tower, the centre of the group of ancient trees and buildings that look down from their commanding site on the roofs and causeways of Culross and on the Firth beyond. Purists in architecture find fault with the Perpendicular battlements, as out of keeping. But the general effect is noble. The present Parish Church occupies the choir of the pre-Reformation structure. It has echoed to much strong Calvinist doctrine since the monks were put to flight. For at Culross Fraser of Brea preached philippics against Prelacy and told of his strange religious 'experiences' while a prisoner for conscience' sake on the Bass; and here, too, Boston of Ettrick and the Erskines sowed the seed of the Secession.

Chapel Barn, Culross.

Standing on the churchyard grass one reads, on the gables of the adjacent aisle and vault, the legend 'Man goeth to his long home,' with the date 1642, and the name 'Sir George Bruce of Carnok, Knight'—the younger of that title. His greater father, the father also of Culross's

prosperity, rests within, under an alabaster tomb
—now the chief mural ornament of the interior
—adorned by figures of his children in the

Culross Abbey Church.

Vandyke costumes of the day. A Bruce that
more attracts the romantic sympathy is young
Edward, Lord Kinloss, who fell in 1613, in
deadly duel fought with Edward Sackville,
Earl of Dorset, in a flooded meadow at Bergen-
op-Zoom. His heart, in its silver casket, reposes
in Culross Kirk.

Close behind the church rise the stately front and pavilion roofs of the mansion of Culross Abbey, a fragment of the magnificent pile begun by the first Lord Kinloss, Master of the Rolls to King James, and designed, as is thought, by his kinsman, the architect-baronet of Kinross. Within it, at a later date, Lord Dundonald, the famous projector, pursued his ingenious but ruinous experiments with coal-tar and naphtha ; while his yet more famous son, the hero of Basque Roads, ran wild about the place and risked his neck bird-nesting in the old pit-shafts. Changed times these since the White Friars patiently copied their illuminated missals, sat in the great Refectory Hall, paced the cloisters, of which a beautiful fragment still bounds the Manse garden, or toiled in the sunny orchard, running down the slope to the burgh confines ; or, in the intervals of work and prayer, watched the sails passing up and down the ' Scots Water,' and the citizens, girdle-smith and maltster-wife, douce burgess and trim damsel, moving through the maze of wynds and terraces between the abbey and the Sandhaven.

When you go back to the foundation of the Cistercian Abbey by Malcolm, Earl of Fife, in 1217, you are not half-way to the beginning of the civil and religious history of Culross. Was not the good Saint Serf teaching his *Scolocs* on this spot in 517, when Saint Thenew was drifted thither from Aberlady, and Saint Kentigern was born? The very spot is known, for on it afterwards rose the little commemorative chapel, erected in 1503, by Archbishop Black adder, the builder of the Blackadder Crypt in St Mungo's Cathedral at Glasgow. And if any one questions the later wonders wrought here by Mungo, the Beloved, as his causing the hazel twig to burst into flame, and his restoring the dead bird to life, are they not

The Cloisters, Culross.

emblazoned—the twig grown into a tree—on the arms of his favoured city of Glasgow, where also his mother, Thenew, has a local habitation and a name as Saint Enoch?

Strolling down the Tanyard Brae from the abbey precincts, we arrest our steps in the open space beside the Cross. The little 'place' is the centre of the burgh. Turn where you like there are groupings of ancient houses with initials, dates, devices, and mottoes carved on gable or door lintel, and vistas of steep and narrow 'Causeways.' Within a few feet of the Cross we note two sixteenth-century dates on the old walls—1577 and 1591. Another quaint edifice, close by the cosy hostelry of the 'Dundonald Arms,' is the reputed residence of the 'Saintly Leighton.' But the most noticeable

and well preserved of the group is the building
with the tall entrance tower, known as 'The
Study.' Here, with our backs to its venerable
vis-à-vis, 'The Ark,' we pause to muse and to
sketch. Its name and story are somewhat of
a mystery. But it is a pleasing fancy that up
that straight and winding stairway, in the
curious little topmost chamber, with winnocks
looking to the different airts of heaven, dwelt
some forgotten scholar, who alternately pored
over his books, watched the stars, and gazed
down, as did the monks before him, on the
gabble and stir of the little bourg.

Any of the 'Cooross Causeys' will lead you
to the Sandhaven and thence to the West Green.
These are cleared spaces by the sea margin where
the inhabitants come to gossip and bask in fine
weather. Doubtless the burgh bailies know
better, but the weather-beaten Tolbooth looks
as if it had not only seen better days, but had
long retired from business. Ranks of old houses
stand here also, under the steep bank, some of
them with tall dormer windows, boldly crowned
with star or thistle finials. Most interesting and
most dilapidated of all are the two ancient
buildings, with the dates 1597 and 1611, which
Culrossians fondly call 'the Palace' or 'the
Colonels' Close.' Here, in the early part of the
eighteenth century, lived the 'Black' and the
'Fair Colonel Erskine.' They were cousins,
and the former was that stern nonjuror and

industrious litigant, John Erskine of Carnock,
to whom has been credited the dying lament :
'I hae ten guid gangin' cases in the Court of
Session, and that idiot, Jock, my son' (the
author of the great Scots law classic, the
Institutes), 'will be settlin' them a' in a month.'

Gaunt, solitary, and dropping to pieces with
age and neglect, they seem, in their fallen estate,
to be screening themselves from the vulgar gaze
behind their courtyard walls. With no little
trouble—for it was not the sight-seeing season—
we persuade the sad-visaged custodier to give
us entry.

'If I let in the like o' you, I micht let in ony-
body,' she says. We fleech and prevail, and are
conducted through the darkling passages and
stairways and mouldering chambers, to the
wagon-roofed room in the older house, which
some artist of three centuries ago has painted
with curious allegorical devices, and with proverbs
in black letter. The damp has nearly obliterated
the colours and designs on one side, but on the
other wall pictures and lettering are still decipher-
able. Culross should take better care of this
Chamber of Imageries and the other curiosities
of the 'Colonels' Close.' Ralph Erskine was
tutor here in the ' Black Colonel's ' time, and with
other 'Marrow Men' must often have handled
the knottier points of Presbyterian doctrine and
discipline under the gaze of the Virtues and
the Sirens ; possibly the germ of the 'Gospel

Sonnets' might be found in these wise old saws teaching constancy and temperance, and the brevity of earthly pomp and pleasure :

All flesh is grass, and withereth like the hay,
And warneth us how well to live, but not how long to stay.

If we may trust Mr Beveridge, the painstaking historian of Culross, these walls may have first been painted to please the eyes of the Modern Solomon, what time he banqueted with the elder Sir George Bruce in the 'collier's house.' We can figure him, curious and fearful, sallying forth, after dejeune, to inspect the marvellous work which his host had constructed for mining the coal underneath the salt water, and how, coming again to the light of day in the sea-girdled 'Moat,' he 'snookit lèse-majestiè,' like the king of like kidney in the 'Yerl o' Watery-deck,' and lustily shouted 'Treason!'

The great Borrowing Days Storm of 1625, in which King James's own light went out, drowned this 'darke, light, pleasant, profitable Hell,' as Taylor the Water Poet had called it, in his style of crazy epigram. The author of the *Pennilesse Pilgrimage* had come hither, drawn, as Defoe and Cobbett were after him, by curiosity and the reputation of the place ; and greatly daring and much wondering he explored Bruce's work :

A long mile thus I past, doune, doune, steepe, steepe,
In deepenesse far more deepe than Neptune's deepe,
While o'er my head (in fourfold stories hie),
Was earth, and sea, and ayre, and sun, and skie.

By the ruins of the 'Moat,' over against the site of 'Macduff's Castle' on Dunimarle, on the Tolbooth steps, or beside Bessie Bar's Well, were a good place to sit and ponder on the fallen fortunes of Culross. A few fowling-punts and pleasure-boats stick in the mud at low water off the little pier, outside which, as records tell us, one hundred and seventy sail would be waiting in the palmy days of the burgh to load coal or salt. The seams are worked out, and the coal-heughs closed. Of Culross's fifty salt-pans not one sends up its smoke. They are things of the past, like the processions carrying green boughs on Saint Serf's Day—like the click of the hand-loom, or the cheerful ring of the girdlesmith's hammer. These leisurely old craftsmen, whose rules directed them to heat and temper the iron 'so that it may last against fire an age or two,' who would not hurry over their work, labouring only three days a week, 'less otherways they should make too many and ill girdles,' could not live in our days of high pressure and cheap and new-fangled invention. First went the monopoly; the girdle followed by and by. The town itself, like the 'honest, worthy, harmless Hell' at the Moat, was drowned by a flood of debt and alien ideas, and little more than the wreck is left. True, it has its modest share of the blessings of modern civilisation. But who shall say that these comforts of old age are amends for the rich blood of youth?

Even the water of Bessie's Spring, by which old Culross folks used to swear, as did the Jews by Jordan, has been tested by the analytic chemist and found wanting. An outland water, brought in pipes, has superseded it, and is doubtless worthy the judgment pronounced by the fishwife on the new Fisherrow supply : 'Wersh stuff, wi' neither taste nor smell.' May not the like be said of the present, when compared with the past, of this and other ancient Fife burghs?

Parting reluctantly from these meditations and from Culross, we follow the shore eastward, past the long line of white cottages of Low Valleyfield. The tide is out, and across the mud-flats and through the haze Preston Island, with its sheaf of ruined walls, looms up like some isle of enchantment. They are but the remains of abandoned coal and salt works. Nothing more romantic clings to them than legends of latter-day smuggling. But they look like the fragments of some mediæval strength or fane, saturated with crime or sanctity. Of all the misfortunes that have fallen on Culross Bay surely the worst were those 'improvements' on Kincardine Moss, far up the river, that have covered the foreshore with black peat ooze. At the bridge over the Bluther Burn we pass the former confines of Perth and Fife. But still the dingy stain of bog-earth and coal-dust soils the fair curves of the beach. Valleyfield, Newmill, and Torryburn

Culross.

were upstart conspirators in the Fifty Years Girdle War that brought their neighbour burgh to naught. Now, as the dates over the doorways tell us, their own best days are past a

Preston Island.

century ago. Good times would return, and the summer bather and tripper would flock to Culross Bay, could only some kind magician exchange its mud for the clean white sands of yore.

At the low green 'ness' of Torry, where the highroad from Dunfermline comes down to the shore, we rest and look back. Here that West of Fife Cotton Mather, the Rev. Allan Logan, may have superintended the tethering of Torry witches below flood-mark. Here the Water Poet got his first glimpse of Culross Bay, as did after him Daniel Defoe, Bishop Pocock, and William Cobbett, all of them travelling towards Alloa. The author of *Rural Rides* was reminded of the shores of Southampton Water and the skirts of the New Forest. Turner, the painter, is said, while a guest of Sir Robert Preston of Valleyfield, to have likened the scene to the Bay of Naples. Such comparisons are fushionless at best. It is our purpose to show that Fife has a native flavour of its own, and is spoiled when served with outlandish sauces.

TORRYBURN TO NORTH QUEENSFERRY.

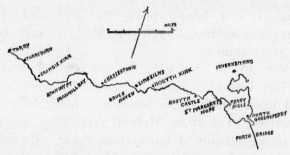

Oh-hoi, ye ho! who's for the Ferry?
The briar's in bud and the sun going down.
Twickenham Ferry.

TIME slips away unheeded in the Sleepy
Hollow of Culross Bay. We have still a
long road to go in the brief winter day to our
haven at North Queensferry. The map does
not show us the position of Old Crombie
Kirk, and the snell air makes us hungry.
We drop into the village inn for information
and refreshment. Its kindly and homely Meg
Dods attends to both wants to the best of her
power.

'Of coorse it's different the like o' us
buddies that kens a' the ways hereabouts, and
goes through a' kind o' places,' she remarks, as
she places on the board the mulled stout and

a noble supply of bread and cheese. And she
proceeds to describe a by-way leading through
the Craigflower grounds. 'We ca' it,' she adds,
critically holding up a plate to the light to spy
for dust, and giving it a finishing polish on the
full part of her dress, 'the Floor Gairden, ye
ken. It's a bonny place, the kirkyaird, but
there's naething there, but kind o' auld bits
o' grave-stanes.'

We go on our way, but do not invade the
'Floor Gairden,' keeping instead by the shore,
out upon which, from beneath a roadside stone
inscribed 'Torryburn Mineral Well, 1893,' gushes
a strong stream of ferruginous water. Crombie
Kirk stands on a height. We climb over the
gateway and drop into the old God's Acre. It
is cumbered with grass-grown mounds and grey
'through' stones and headstones, the resting-
places of dead and gone shipmasters and salt-
makers, artisans and 'mediciners.' Some bear
the insignia of their craft—here a quadrant and
there a hammer. In the centre is the ivy-clad
ruin of the little church, in former times, with
the whole of the ancient parish of Crombie, a
possession of the monks of Culross. It has
been roofless these two centuries and a half,
and looks a likely place for the trysts of the
Torryburn witches. Along the south side of
the churchyard are a line of tall yews—ghostly
sentinels keeping watch to seaward. In that
direction there opens a bewitching view of the

Firth and of the shores of Fife and Lothian, and this we enjoy, with many changes of angle and foreground as we follow for a couple of miles the woodland walks skirting the steep brae-face and leading past Crombie Point, with its handful of houses and unfrequented little stone landing-pier, to the western horn of Ironmill Bay.

It is tame after Culross. But looking across it, Charlestown Harbour, overhung by the Broomhall woods, and with the masts and yards of its shipping forming a criss-cross pattern against the members of the great Bridge, looks a picturesque enough object. Reaching it, we find a tangle of railway sidings, with coal and lime trucks and stacks of pit-props, an outer and inner basin crowded with steamers and foreign sailing craft, and, facing the quay, a line of cyclopean draw-kilns and a shipchandler's shop. There is a village and village green, we learn, on the bank above, but as Charlestown and its mineral and shipping-trade are little more than a century old, we do not climb to see.

There is metal more attractive close by, at Limekilns. For a bold green background it has the cliffs and woods of Broomhall, the seat of the Bruces, Earls of Elgin, the much-loved early home of Lady Augusta Stanley, where among other cherished relics are kept Bruce's sword, with which Robert Burns was sportively 'knighted' by a descendant of the hero of

Bannockburn, and the bed in which Charles I. was born. The lean white houses of the village crouch below the flag-staffed 'Gellet Rock'— a relic of the old limestone workings—and seem to stare ruefully into the deserted harbour in search of the trade that has left and does not promise to return again in a hurry. The business of Limekilns was chiefly in the past. It owned once forty sail of coasting and sea-going craft, and employed one hundred and sixty ship-carpenters; and it boasts the ruins of the oldest of the salt-pans on the Forth. Now it cultivates the summer boarder. But in the winter, time seems to hang heavily on its hands; even the defaced sun-dials on the corners of the eaves speak of neglect of the passing hour.

Up a little side street, and close under the cliff, an ancient building catches the eye. It is the 'King's Cellar'—the 'Vout,' in local nomenclature — where, haply, the 'bluid-red wine' and other foreign delicacies were stored as they came from shipboard, when our Scottish Kings sat in Dumfermline Tower, and where, as has been said (but is questioned), Commendator Pitcairne died, having come 'sick out of Flanders,' to meet the pest at Limekilns. There is an outside stair leading to the upper floor, and above it protrude the ribs of the vaulted roof. The date, 1581, which accompanies the heraldic shield bearing the arms of Pitcairne and Murray, above the doorway,

belies a little the story of its great antiquity
and traditional use; it may be a later intrusion
commemorative of the marriage of the Commendator, whose tomb is in Dunfermline
Abbey, with Euphane Murray of Tullibardine.

A voice from an entry tells us to 'go down
the first close and up the second stair' for the
key. The injunction is obeyed, and a buxom
lass, kilted for housework—such like as she
who brought comfort and succour here to
David Balfour and Allan Breck Stewart—
presents herself.

'It's nae use,' she says, on hearing the
request; and in answer to a mute appeal
for enlightenment, she adds, 'it's awa wi't.'
Further explanation being asked, she continues,
'Ye'll be for haddin' a public meetin'?' When
it is known that we only want a peep inside,
her father is summoned. With the aid of this
old residenter we gain admission to the building, and find ourselves in a long and lofty
vaulted chamber. Two splayed windows are
cut through a great thickness of wall, but one
of them is boarded up, and the high-pitched
Gothic roof is lost in shadow. A couple of
rough forms are drawn up on each side of an
old table, on which are two battered candle-
sticks holding guttered dips. It is like a hall
in the 'Chateau of Misery,' this mildewed woebegone place. But it had been used, after
its fortunes began to decline, as a school,

which Limekilns 'ca'd an Academy'; and, as we discover by candle light, a part of the eastern end had once been partitioned off as the 'Public Library.'

'Naebody comes here langer,' we are told, 'but the remains o' the auld Beerial Society; and little they've left to do except beery ane anither.' The table and other properties belong, it appears, to this antique remnant. It were worth while to watch them as they pore over their funeral account books, with the candle light throwing up grotesque shadows on walls and roof.

Outside, our ancient guide informs us that his father-in-law minded when there was another storey to the King's Cellar; 'he could tell ye a' aboot it,' he adds. A lost and improbable tale. We inquire with interest where this venerable authority is to be found. 'In Rosyth; he's deid, of coorse,' is the reply, not without a touch of the Fifer's wonder at the ignorance of the stranger.

Rosyth churchyard is on a spur of the coast, half a mile to the east of Brucehaven. As has been said, those tiny and ancient burial-grounds on the sea margin are characteristic of the fringes of Fife. One at least we have already come upon, and there are many ahead —Dalgety, Kinghorn, St Monans, and others. But perhaps there is none more lonely and eerie than Rosyth, at any rate at the close of a

winter day, when a rising wind is soughing
through the bare branches, and the sea is
beginning to moan and tramp to and fro over
rock and shingle. A little grove of trees sur-
rounds and shelters it on the land side. Elsewhere the Firth is its boundary, and from the
beach you climb over the stile into the
churchyard. Of the church all that remains is
the ruined north wall and the east gable,
pierced by two graceful lancet windows, half
screened by ivy. In the gathering dusk we
spell out the inscriptions, and note how many
who now sleep soundly to the lapping of the
waves were of those who go down to the sea
in ships and do business on the mighty waters.
In this restful nook are garnered up all the
life and movement of past generations of Limekilns and the country round—rough mariners
who made many a stormy voyage to Campvere
and Bergen and Nantes without paying kain
to the sea; and dour and stern-faced weavers
and salters who have trudged weary miles
inland to the ' Holy Fair ' of Carnock to listen
to the preaching of Row, or, long after, to
partake of the marrow of Gillespie's communion
exhortations, or have climbed the Hill of Beath
to hear from the lips of Mr John Blackadder
the story of his sufferings at the hands of
men of Belial.

The churchyard of Rosyth is a choice place
to moralise over the vanity of the race for gold,

and the strifes of sects and factions.   So, also,
is the courtyard of Rosyth Castle.   The sun
had set behind an angry bank of cloud when
we reached the tall grim keep rising from the
green island, joined by a causeway to the land.

Rosyth Castle.

Here, some tell us, at the 'landing-place of the
headland,' Margaret, Saint and Queen, with her
brother the Atheling, her mother and sister,
and the refugee Anglian lords, may have stepped
ashore, after finding shelter in St Margaret's
Hope, to be received with open arms by Malcolm
Greathead, and to change the course of Scottish
and Fifish history.   Here, five hundred years
later, as seems partly attested by the date 1561
and the initials 'M. R.' above the portal, Mary

Stuart rested on one of her many journeys through Fife. Cromwell's mother is said to have been of the family of the Stewarts of Rosyth, and Carlyle tells us that the genealogists have indubitably proved that Oliver was 'the fractional part of half a cousin' of the Royal Martyr. Little the stern-souled Protector recked of sentimental reasons for sparing the place when, from the other side of the Forth he watched his troopers battering the keep, after his army had stolen a march across the Ferry and gained for him his 'unspeakable mercy' on the hills behind Inverkeithing.

It is too dark—even had the stone still been in place—to read the hospitable legend said to have been written over the doorway that enters from the courtyard :

In . dev . tym . dra . yis . cord . ye . bel . to . clink .
Quhais . mery . voce . warnis . to . mete . and . drink .

There is little of mirth or welcome in the present aspect of the ancient hold. The light from the western sky is drawn like a smear of red fingers across the mullions of the great tower and the broken edges of the chapel walls ; and the tide pools around seem filled with 'lappered bluid.'

At the 'loanhead of Rosyth' an abbot of Culross was foully slain by the Laird of Tulli-allan, with the help of a monk of his own convent. He was Sir James Inglis, a 'makar' of

plays and satires in high repute at the court
of James IV. Sir David Lyndesay says of him :

> Who can say more than Sir James Inglis says
> In ballads, farces, and in pleasant plays.
> But Culross hath his pen made impotent.

He gave up his ballad-making to superintend
the copyists of psalters and breviaries, and to
fall into deadly feud with the Blackadders.

From the Loanhead we hie us by road
towards the neck of the peninsula, and over
the gusty Ferry Hills. The wind and the
stars are out, and on such a night the fancy
likes to dally with what might have been, as
well as with what was and is. The Jews, it is
said, were once in treaty with Alexander III.
to purchase this promontory and build on it
their city of refuge. Golf is played on the
plateau where the synagogues might have
been pitched ; the railway, the main line of
traffic between North and South, burrows and
quarries beside the track once followed by the
pilgrims on their way to St Margaret's Shrine.
At length we look down upon the many lights
twinkling in the village of North Queensferry
and gleaming far out on the water. Above us
the Forth Bridge hangs like a huge and dusky
cobweb stretched across the mile of firth, and
fastened midway on Inchgarvie. Roy of
Aldivalloch once held the island fort with a
company of Royalist musketeers, until turned

out by General Lambert. It is now used to
signal to passing vessels the waterways under
the great cantilevers. As we look the new
spirit of the scene comes sweeping with roar
and flame across the centre of its iron web,
and plunges into its cavern; and we step downward to the rest and solace of our inn.

INVERKEITHING TO BURNTISLAND.

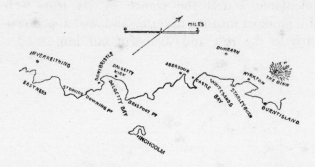

Let's talk of graves, and worms, and epitaphs. —*Richard II.*

AT Inverkeithing, hunkering on its hillside looking towards the south-east, we light down on one of the rare mornings in a season of wet and storm when the sun shines out brightly if briefly before mid-day. In this light the spacious main street of the burgh puts on a cheerful air. But it has a patched and clouted look; as of something old and substantial that has been repaired with more flimsy materials. The heavy stone forestairs, the arched or moulded doorways, and the tiled roofs, corbie-stepped at the gables and bearing tiers of windows and chimneys between eaves and ridge, do not compose well with the modern bank and shop-front.

Looking eastward the vista is closed by the Parish Church, dedicated to St Peter; and it may well be taken as an epitome of the burgh architecture. It has a long history, having been gifted to the Abbey of Dunfermline in 1126 by Waldeve, the son of the great Earl Gospatrick of Dunbar. The weather-battered western tower, middle-pointed in style, is nearly all that remains of the pre-Reformation Church; and it has been furnished with a tasteless and incongruous doorway and capped by a modern clock-spire. The body of the building has been thrice burned; the church was last rebuilt in 1826, and, considering the taste of the time, the interior is better than one might have looked for. The chief curiosity of St Peter's is its ancient font, a perfect example of its kind and date, decorated with six panels containing boldly blazoned shields supported by flat-faced angels with curled locks. It has been preserved and restored to its original use more 'by luck than guid guiding.' The bowl was found early in the century buried in straw under the entrance porch below the tower, and it was fitted to the pedestal which had lain neglected in the churchyard. Within it were bones—evidently relics, for the sake of which the font had been hid away; an irreverent and ungrateful age cast them forth.

On the north side of the street stood, till lately, two venerable buildings with roundel towers. One has been cleared away—old houses,

like old bones, must give place. The other,
sadly battered by time and ill-usage, still holds
its place opposite the Kirk door. Says the good
woman who had shown us through St Peter's,
'There's a wheen poor folk in the riggin', and
the Mission Hall's below. It's no considered
safe for onything else,' she naïvely adds. We
climb up and look in on the 'poor folk'; they
are affable if clarty. 'Fine, hoo are ye yersels;
come awa ben,' is the response to our greeting.
'This was Clavers's hoose, and here's whaur the
king sleepit,' we are told; 'and here' (leading
the way to the roundel
turret) 'was whaur they
keepit the spies.'

Inverkeithing Town Hall.

There are two islands
of houses in the high
street of Inverkeithing.
One is at the east end,
where the thoroughfare
forks, sending a branch
up the slope past the
church, and another
down the hill towards the
Keithing burn; it screens
the pepper-box tower of
the Town House and
the handsome shaft, with a heraldic capital surmounted by a unicorn, of the ancient Town
Cross. The other is at the west end; like a
breakwater it seems to shelter from the impact

Pettycur Pier—Inchcolm on left, Burntisland on right.

of modern influences the great rambling fabric behind known as Rothmells Inn.

The vast expanse of white wall turned to the little back street has a window dotted here and there ; and built against it are two huge outer stairs. Symmetry has been set at naught in every line, exterior and interior, of this structure, built, we are told, to be a Queen's palace ; and we like it all the better for its manifold irregularities and surprises. Queen Annabella Drummond is the only one of its many royal guests and residents of whom Inverkeithing retains a definite memory ; perhaps because her dwelling was placed outside of burgh jurisdiction, and the magistrates were bound to pay her one hundred shillings on Pentecost Day. She was of the Drummonds of Stobhall, a family famed for the loveliness of feature and complexion of their women, and, as old Holinshed states, she was married rather for her singular beauty 'than for anie benefit that might grow to the Commonwealth from her alliance.' Yet has history a good word to say of her domestic virtues and of her prudence in counsel. Great sorrows visited her in Inverkeithing ; of her two sons, David, Duke of Rothesay, was foully done to death at Falkland, and James I., the Poet King, fell under the assassins' daggers in the Blackfriars Monastery at Perth. Local tradition, ever fanciful, would give her other griefs. It pictures her as a forsaken Queen, sitting at her bower window, where

she could gaze across the reaches of the bay and
Firth to where the rock and castle of Edinburgh
seem to hang half in air.

> Oh, waly! waly! love be bonnie
> A little while when it is new;
> But when it's auld it waxeth cauld
> And fades awa like mornin' dew.

King Robert III. was a weak prince, but he
was neither bad man nor faithless husband; and
the beautiful mistress of Rothmells Inn may have
looked with calmer eyes and happier thoughts
on the bitter and restless waters sundering her
from Court than did other minions of fortune
who afterwards watched from this portion of the
fringes of Fife the scene of their former pomp
and power. The 'Queen's Chambers' are a
quaint set of rooms, from the first of which you
plunge down a few steps into what may have
been the boudoir, or ascend not less abruptly to
the sleeping apartment overhead. The former
is vaulted, and has other two windows besides
the arched and now half-built-up casement opening on the sea and the south; and both rooms
command a prospect worthy of the eyes of a
beautiful queen. The grand old kitchen, also
vaulted, with the huge fireplace, and the light
coming in over the doorway through an immense
thickness of solid wall, should not be missed.

Behind there is a well-kept space of ground
sloping down towards the shore, and in it are
a range of ecclesiastical vaults that may have

belonged to the Franciscan Monastery; or they may be remains of the Queen's oratory. All

Queen Annabella Drummond's House.

the old houses on this sunny side of the Inverkeithing main street have their long gardens running downhill, with high walls, and here and there an ancient doocot separating them from the turbid waters of the burn and the muddy harbour, which the ebbing tide is leaving bare.

As we linger a rain squall comes blattering over the Ferry Hills, darkening the sky and hiding the sun. This, after all, is the right light in which to view Inverkeithing. It has not fulfilled the bright promise of its morning. It has itself played for centuries the part of the deserted favourite, and watched trade and importance drift away from it down the Firth and across the water. No burgh royal of the Kingdom had a better or earlier start. In its younger years privileges and honours fairly rained on it. 'King David I. dwell'd sometime in it; in King William's reign it flourished much,' says the learned but not too accurate Sibbald. It is certain that later sovereigns halted at it often on their journeys by sea and land, and signed there charters and decrees. It had power of pit and gallows; the Provost had the right of riding next to the Chief Magistrate of Edinburgh at the meeting of the Scottish Estates; it owned jurisdiction from the Devon to the Leven, took toll of all the ships that passed through the narrows, and collected fair dues and customs as far inland as Kinross. Nor were Church favours wanting. The Culdees, that mysterious religious order which seems to have had its beginning and end in Fife, are said to have held their last assemblage at Inverkeithing. Monasteries of the White and Black Friars afterwards took the place, and probably the property, of the monks of the old rule.

This day the good town seems half-asleep, and such of the inhabitants as we speak to only half awake, as we leave it and skirt the oozy margin of the bay, fast emptying with the ebb-tide. The only sound is the clatter of the riveters' hammers in the shipbuilding yard; and this dies away before we reach the spot where the crescent horns of Inverkeithing Bay approach each other at the East and the West Ness—the latter formerly a quarantine station and lazaretto house, and afterwards put to more cheerful use as sea-bathing quarters.

Keeping the shore path for St Davids, another pelting rain shower overtakes us, and we flee for shelter to a wooden shed facing the sea and the blast. Towards us come two grave-faced men, an elder and a younger, the former with a sack round his shoulders, while the other bears an iron pail.

'Ye'll hae mair elbowroom and less weet inside,' they civilly remark to us, standing in the slushy doorway. 'We'll need a' the licht.'

We give place.

'Whammle the pail, Richie,' says he of the sack. The pail is whammled where the mud was ankle-deep; he sits down, and his companion, producing a huge tailor's shears, proceeds in solemn silence to prune his locks, as if hair-cutting in a rain squall on a lonely sea-shore, out of hail of human habitation, were the most ordinary thing in life. But strange things happen in Fife.

Before the operation is over the rain has eased off, and we move round by the little coaling-port of St Davids and begin to trace the Donibristle shore. Here the Fife coast is scalloped into deep bays and bold headlands, off which are sprinkled islands and stacks of sea-washed rock. Trees fringe the bights and crown most of the promontories that run their black noses out into the water; and behind are the lawns and groves of a noble demesne. It is a winding way to follow the shore, but each turn in it brings some delightful surprise.

Behind the sharp snout of Downing Point, on a curving platform overlooking the Firth, we come on what the fire has left of Donibristle House. It has 'dreed its weird' by being thrice burned. The last time was in 1858, and it has never been rebuilt. The walls of the central block of building, in the Queen Anne style, stand up gaunt and desolate. Time has not yet—and probably never will—put any beautifying touch on them or on the dismal mortuary chapel in the clump of trees behind, where the Earls of Moray are buried. The two wings are at a much lower level, and are intact. There is no above-ground connection,

but the smooth green turf, bounded to seaward
by a staircase descending to the shore, and by
a magnificent decorative gateway of old Dutch
hammered work, presented by 'Great Anna'
to a Lady Moray in the first year of the
eighteenth century, sounds hollow underfoot.
It is honey-combed with underground passages ;
and thereby hangs the tale of Donibristle—the
tragedy of the 'Bonnie Earl o' Moray.' That
was in the time of the first burning, in 1592.
Of the braw gallant himself we know little that
is admirable, beyond his 'weel-faured face.'
But he was the son-in-law of that Regent
Moray whom his friends called the 'Good,'
and for whom his enemies had another name.
You can still see at Donibristle the beautiful
old carved oak chair, bearing his initials. In
it, a generation earlier, the Regent sat grimly
awaiting news of the murder of Darnley, in
which, like his neighbour and successor in
power, Morton, he is suspected of being 'art
and part.' The Bonnie Earl was sib to the
King and a leader of the Protestant faction ;
while his murderers were in the other boat, and
mixed afterwards in the Spanish Blanks and
other dark intrigues of the time ; and thus the
business took a strong hold of the popular
mind :

> Ye Hielands and ye Lowlands,
>   Oh whaur hae ye been !
> They 've slain the Yerl o' Moray
>   That sud ha been the King.

Some obscure blood-letting up in the north
was the beginning of the feud with the Gordons;
although the people's suspicions ran in another
channel.

> The Bonnie Yerl o' Moray
> He was the Queen's love.

In pursuit of his revenge, Lord Huntley
started from Edinburgh late on a February
evening, and, crossing at Queensferry with his
company, set fire to the unprotected and un-
garrisoned House of Donibristle. It was then
that Sheriff Dunbar, the ' Tutor of Moray,' gave
his rare proof of devotion to the death. For
the Earl, ' wissing not quhither to come out
and be slaine or be burned quicke,' the Tutor
volunteered to go first out of the gate so that
(said he) ' the peopell will chairge on me,
thinking me to be your lordshipe; sae, it being
mirke under nycht; ye sall come out after me
and look if that ye can fend for yourself.'
Dunbar fell under the weapons of the Gordons,
and Murray escaped by the subterranean passage
leading through the eastern pavilion to the
shore, and sat down among the rocks to draw
breath. But, by ill hap, according to the quaint
relation in Birrell's *Diary*, ' the said lord's cnap-
scull tippet quherone ves a silk stringe had
taken fyre, vich betrayed him to his enimies
in ye darknesse of ye nycht,' and they were
upon him before he knew. Gordon of Buckie
gave the deadly wound, and Huntly himself,

it is said, slashed the face of the dying man, who turned upon him with the words, 'You've spoiled a better face than your own.'

The blood of the young Earl—he was but four-and-twenty years of age—cried long in vain for vengeance, although his mother had the corpse borne on a bier two days later from Leith to St Giles Kirk, with a banner (still preserved at Donibristle) whereon was painted the naked body and its wounds, with the device 'God Avenge my Cause.' One touch of sweet ruth and charity there is in this dark tale of blood. For Captain John Gordon of Gicht, left for dead at the gate of Donibristle by his own party (after they had stripped him), was taken in and 'cherished with meat, drink, and clothing' by the dead Earl's mother. Truly a strange compound of savage and of noble qualities were those men and women of three centuries ago!

The home-farm of Donibristle is the scene of a reputed victory won by Sinclair, the 'Fechting Bishop' of Dunkeld, over the English in the time of the War of Independence. A better authenticated act of heroism took place here in the summer before the Waterloo year. Robert Moffat, the missionary, was employed as a journeyman in the Donibristle gardens, and he nearly lost his own life in rescuing that of a fellow-workman who was on the point of drowning in the Forth off the little quay.

Round the next turn of the coast we come
on Dalgety Bay. The shore curves like a bent
bow, and at the centre of the arc is Old Dalgety
Kirk. A brook tumbles out on the beach on
one side of the churchyard wall, and the old
kirk road dips to the sea on the other. So
secluded is the nook, and so closely are the
trees set about the roofless grey walls of St
Bridget's Church, that you are close under them
before you are aware they are near. Even
then you have to look twice before you are
sure whether it is a ruined mansion or a 'Kirk
deserted by its riggin'' that is hid away here
by the sea-shore. At the western end rise a
sheaf of gables—two crowned by crescents, a
third by a belfry and bell, with the mark of
the bell-rope cut deep into the stone, and a
fourth by a chimney. By a turnpike stair you
ascend to the sacristy. It is a room panelled
with moulded stone, and has a snug sanctum
with a fireplace beyond. You love to believe,
as a mark of grace and Christian charity in an
age of ejected ministers and rabbled curates,
the story of the Presbyterian pastor who was
allowed by the kind-hearted 'Prelatic' appointed
in his stead to shelter for twenty years his head
here in the Killing Time.

A church, successor to a Culdee cell, has
stood on this spot for more than seven hundred
years. The ivy is busy tugging down the
eastern gable. Built into the inside wall is a

fine slab, inscribed in boldly raised characters
to 'Ane honorabil man callit Villiam Abernethe
of Dagati,' with the date '1540.' A later
possessor was that great pluralist and sagacious

Dalgety Church.

lawyer and statesman, Chancellor Seton, Earl
of Dunfermline, to whose charge the Modern
Solomon committed the care of the princes,
Henry and Charles. He was buried at Dalgety
in 1622, in the vault under the priest's chamber,
with great state. A contemporary description
of the funeral mentions, among the lugubrious
paraphernalia of grief, 'Ane Morthead, painted
on black Tefety, Poudered with teares, on a

speir's poynt.' The nobility of the Kingdom were assembled at 'ye good Kirk or Chappell at ye Seaside,' and 'an excellent Sermone was maid by Mr Spotswood, Archbishope of St Andrews.' One of the last to preach in Old Dalgety Church was Edward Irving.

All trace of the Chancellor's 'Place of Dalgety,' and of Dalgety village, has disappeared. The birds of the air and of the sea have now undisputed possession. A flight of mallard springs squattering from the shallower waters as we tramp the lonely shore towards Braefoot Point. Sandpipers rise and light again among the wreckage heaped up by the westerly gales. From under the group of low gnarled pines on the headland, writhing and grovelling as if in agony, a sooty-grey water-hen starts up, and, trailing its green legs, makes a sweep back again to cover. Off the ruddy-brown rocks of basalt that stretch out towards Inchcolm razorbills and guillemots bob and dive.

Travellers were not always such ferlies on this track. The Abbots of Inchcolm had a residence and grange at Donibristle. The canons and choristers of that 'nocht obskure monastar,' as Bishop Lesley calls it, served Dalgety Kirk; and there were many passings to and fro across the dangerous mile of firth.

To-day we cross not Mortimer's Deep; Inchcolm is but a bit of hazy background in our picture of Fife. But resting beside the old monks' landing-place and looking across the mile-broad reach of sea that separates us from the square grey tower that shows against the sky from the sheltered hollow in the 'island salt and bare,' we almost seem to hear again the chime of the Abbey bells, silent for centuries, borne across the water. There is a briny flavour and an air of miracle about Inchcolm and all its memories. It was Æmonia before it was St Colme's Inch ; the Druid's Isle before being 'the Isle of Saints.' The sea-robbers vexed it long before, and long after, the time recorded by Shakespeare, when 'Sweno, Norway's King,' disbursed on it ten thousand dollars to Macbeth and Banquo for right of sepulture to his men. It was in 1123 that Alexander the Fierce, caught in a storm while crossing, on affairs of State, to Inverkeithing, was glad to crawl ashore and find shelter with its hermit, probably in the rude stone-roofed oratory that remains until this day. He found more lenten entertainment than the Black Knight met with from the Clerk of Copmanhurst—dulse, cockles, and the milk of the 'ae coo' that grazed the island. But in gratitude he founded a priory of Augustinian canons-regular ; which was afterwards endowed with rich gifts, among others by that Mortimer, Lord of Aberdour, whose body the monks dropped overboard in the channel that still bears his name. They kept his lands, but would have none of his bones.

For the rest, the patron saint—if this, as has been doubted, was 'Colum of the Church,' and not the milder St Colman—looked jealously after the interests of his shrine and island so long as the Old Religion prevailed. The monks of Derry and Iona knew Columba in life as a 'man of strife,' dangerous to cross; and if we may believe the marvels related by Abbot Bowmaker, Fordun's continuator, who wrote his *Scotichronicon* in the Scriptorium of Inch-colm, the same imperious temper marked his post-mortem guardianship. English sea-reivers, who pillaged the Abbey lands and carried away the Abbey plate and valuables, were sent, ship and man, to the bottom of the Firth by the irate Saint, or were visited by storms and aches and misfortunes until they were glad to return and do penance. Well might the ancient mariners dub him St Qualm! But he was powerless to avenge himself on the greedy hands that at the Reformation snatched at the Abbey itself and all its possessions; and Inchcolm de-generated into a pirate's hold, a fortification, and a lazaretto; and so faded out of history. It was a spot after the heart of the bold and solitary spirit who sang of his delight 'in the salt sea, where the sea-gulls cry.'

> To sit on the pinnacle of the rock
> That I might often look
> On the face of ocean;
> That I might hear the thunder of the crowding
> waves
> Upon the rocks;
> The roar by the side of the church
> Of the surrounding sea.

Half-an-hour later we are standing in the outer solitude of the main street of Aberdour. The life and movement of the gusty March day are shut in behind the big gates of Donibristle— the flashes of white, from breaking waves or sea-birds' wings, that come and go among the shore rocks; the blackbirds and chaffinches, busy in the walks and coppices; the rooks balancing on the high bare branches and interrupting, with their noisy discussion of the great housing question, the sough of the wind in the beech-trees.

Looking eastward along the deserted village highway the only objects visible are a wheel-barrow standing before a door, and a pump swathed in straw against the frost. Those who pay it only fair-weather summer visits do not rightly know their Aberdour. They should come hither in the drear season on the debatable line of winter and spring, when they can have it all to themselves. Not a tripper lingers under the shade of the beeches by the Silver Sands, or watches from the outlook on the Hawkcraig the coming and going of the steamers at the pier below. The pleasure-craft are hauled up high and dry beyond the mud of the little harbour ; and the Tea Gardens are a desolation.

By and by, as you watch from the windows of the village inn—chosen on grounds of character and not of style—the village types, who creep out of sight when strangers are about, come forth ; the sleepy village life circulates. A chain of carts clatters along the street, bringing heads to the doors and windows ; a tramp or a commercial traveller's gig brings whiffs of outside influence and excitement. In the old days, when, instead of being invaded by crowds of summer bathers and loungers it was the resort of pilgrims to its Holy Well, Aberdour had probably the same alternating periods of stir and rest. It has lost all trace of its waters of healing, and no longer knows even the site of the nunnery of sisters of St Francis—the Hospital of St Martha— established in the Easter village by a pious Countess of Morton for the entertainment of poor travellers. The water of the Pilgrims' Well was a sovereign remedy for sore eyes.

Aberdour is still a ' sicht for sair een.' Its great charm and virtue are in its situation. Its bay is a dimple of beauty in the stern lineaments of Fife ; and lovely it remains, even in March weather, and after the railway has drawn an ugly scratch across its wooded slopes.

Narrowly has the line missed rooting up the foundations of the Castle, nodding to its ruin over the dell of the Dour. To-day it expresses

Town Hall, Dysart.

5

three ages of neglect and decay. At the western
end is the ancient keep. The flail of the winds
has mercilessly pounded the strong walls, and
great fragments have rolled down the slope

Aberdour Castle.

towards the burn. Within, dark and noisome
weeds make the ruin hideous as well as melancholy. The central portion of the Castle is of
later date. There is a long gallery on the upper
floor still roofed over, and filled from end to end
with hay. Access is got to it by a roundel tower
and newel stair from the courtyard behind, and

F.F. 5

its windows overlook towards the south the narrow garden and bowling alley, screened by their high wall, and beyond these the smooth green slopes descending to the bay and the Firth. The chamber had been used as a public school and as cavalry barracks before descending to the estate of a hay-loft. The eastern wing is dilapidated enough, but still habitable and inhabited. The style and the date (1635) on the fine old circular sun-dial near the southern doorway indicate that this part of the building was erected in the time of William, Earl of Morton, who spent his all in the cause of the First Charles. A healthy family of youngsters are at their meal in the room where, we are told, there is a fine painted ceiling of the same period. But it is papered over and white-washed. The present owners of the Castle seem to have no care or interest in the pile that has been in the hands of the family through good and evil fortune for four hundred years, and 'they'll no put in a pane o' glass,' we hear.

We borrow a little girl to guide us to the ancient Church of Aberdour, standing close under the Castle walls. 'Do the ghosts disturb you?' we ask, as she fumbles at the lock of the old orchard. 'Na; they never come near us,' she tells us gravely. Doubtless they are content with their own wide and growing territory within the Castle walls, and avoid the remote nook where there is still a spark of human life and warmth.

> The leal Guidman o' Aberdour
> Sits in Sir Alan Vipont's tower,

and on moonlight nights watches the elves dance on the greensward below, whence they spirited away the baron's daughter to the land of Faëry. After the Viponts followed the Mortimers. The Regent Randolph was a later possessor, and gifted the Cullalo Hills, whose dark wooded ridge, stretching away towards Dunearn Hill and the Binn of Burntisland, fend Aberdour from the north winds, to the monks of Dunfermline, to sing masses for the soul of his uncle, the Bruce. The Douglases, Earls of Morton, of the doughty line of the Knight of Liddesdale, came next, and last. If any unquiet ghost inhabit these ruins, it must be that of the Regent Morton—Regents were rife of old in this strip of Fife. That type of the rapacious and unscrupulous time-server of his age sought this retreat in Fife, after his fall from power had driven him from Holyrood and Dalkeith. He was the inventor of the Tulchan Bishop and of the Maiden ; and his own neck, it is said, was among the first on which the new heading-knife descended. More than his own soul he loved to gather gold and heap stone on stone. He was executed for being accessory to the tragedy of Kirk o' Field, and for clipping the King's coin. One can easily fancy the

perturbéd spirit of the man of blood girning
and glowering across the Firth from the empty
windows of Aberdour, and muttering the curse
of one of his kin—

> Edinburgh Castle, town and tower,
>   God grant you sink for sin;
> And that even for the black dinoure,
>   Earl Douglas gat therein—

or haunting the spot, never yet found by any
treasure-seeker, where, under the 'braid stane
before the gate of Aberdour,' his ill-gotten wealth
is hid.

Fig-trees still grow against the high orchard
walls facing the west and south, and in their
withered fruit our guide takes more interest
than in ghosts. 'There was a ripe ane last
year,' she confides to us—one last memory,
enticed to life by the sun of a warm summer,
of Aberdour's Age of Gold.

A key to the enclosure of St Fillan's Church
is not forthcoming, and we clamber over. Thus,
like thieves in the night, have we to climb the
walls of most of these old Fife churchyards; and
here the feat is complicated by barbed wire.
Could not the simple device of a stile be provided, so that in order to meditate among the
tombs one need not run the risk of bruised limbs
and torn clothes? Perhaps not one in a thousand
of Aberdour's visitors wanders into this green
and quiet nook. The loss is theirs. Hidden
although it be among grey walls and shadow-

ing trees, it has an airy lookout over one of the loveliest landscapes in Fife. Beyond the gentle swell and fall of the lawns descending to the burn and the harbour, there is a glimpse of the Firth and its islands, framed by the cliffs and trees of the Hawkcraig and of Cuttle-hill, this last crowned by an obelisk raised by the lords of Aberdour as a landmark by which their Fife seat might be seen from their Lothian home at Dalmahoy. Here may one glance cheerfully abroad upon a beautiful world, or brood on tombs, and worms, and epitaphs. The village is shut out by the screen of walls and trees. The crumbling castle and the doocot are the nearest neighbours of the church.

It is a venerable but composite fabric, con-taining a nave communicating through a Norman doorway with a chancel, and separated by three fine semicircular arches of wide span from what was the south aisle. Huge trees, the roots of which still cumber the nave, have had time to grow up since the church was unroofed.[1] The Pilgrims' Well sprang from close below the churchyard wall before it was drained and buried out of sight and memory ('Thrift, thrift, Horatio!').

Built into the wall of the aisle is the tomb-stone of that unflinching Covenanter, the Rev. Robert Blair, minister of the Town Church of St Andrews—colleague of Rutherford, and

[1] All this is now changed, the church having been restored.

adversary of Sharp—whom the Archbishop hunted out of St Rule's as far as Couston in this neighbourhood, where he died, worn out with labours of body and spirit. It was he who dubbed Cromwell 'a greetin' deevil,' and who, after he had been chaplain to Charles I., reproved his wife (says legend) because she offered a chair in the manse to that unsatisfactory specimen of a Covenanting king, the Merry Monarch: so exacting was the Puritan conscience of the day. The author of *The Grave* was his grandson and namesake, and from this stern saint and presbyter have sprung other celebrated Blairs—lawyers, divines, rhetoricians, and men of science. A tablet to the Listons, father and son, ministers for many years of the parish, reminds us, too, that the forebears of the famous surgeon, Robert Liston, sleep at Aberdour.

It is time to be climbing walls again, and making our way through the grove of magnificent beeches and sycamores belting the 'Silver Sands.' On the hill above is Humbie farm, where Carlyle rested or wrestled on his way through 'the valley of the Shadow of Frederick'; on the strand below, it is feigned, Sir Patrick Spens, of the grand old ballad, paced with the 'braid letter' in his hand that sent him on his fateful voyage 'to Norrowa' over the faem.' The footpath winds onward, round the elbows and curves of the coast towards Burntisland, now full in sight beyond the woods of Rossend

Castle, with Inchkeith showing clear outside.
In other days there would have been more
temptation to loiter over this part of the road.
In other days the path wound up and down
a brae-face clothed with wood, and in and out

Rossend Castle Gateway.

among rocks and trees. The railway has passed
this way, scoring and flaying the hillside. For
moss and ivy and wild-flowers one is offered
the recompense of a good level track bounded
by solid stone and lime. It is still a beautiful
walk; but to enjoy it one must forget what
has been. The views to seaward cannot be

spoiled; but the alternate light and shadow of the foreground, the glory of the Hewes Woods, has vanished.

And so we come to Starleyburn, with its waterfall and petrifying spring and little harbour, where formerly 'the King's ships came to water,' a practice which, one would think, must have formed large deposits of lime in the 'inwards' of the royal navy. Finally to Burnt-island, 'waiting'—as wrote the Lord Protector from this *Portus Salutis*, in the middle of the seventeenth century—'waiting what way God will further lead us.'

BURNTISLAND TO KIRKCALDY.

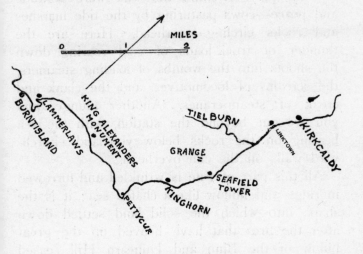

Burntisland for salted herring,
Kinghorn for cursing and swearing.

Fife Saying.

Cockly Carcawdy, facing the sea.

Richard Franck, 1656.

AFTER having approached Burntisland in many ways and in all weathers, by sea and by land, we decide that the praise for dramatic effect belongs to entry by rail from the west. It is like the shifting of scenes in a theatre. You are traversing green meadows down by the sea, which winds a loving arm around the peninsula of Rossend and stretches

73

a finger through the hollow land towards the Kirkton, when suddenly you have broken through a thin partition of rock and are crossing the space where a broad thoroughfare meets a busy quay. Behind the wall were solitude and peace—cows pasturing by the tide marshes and rooks circling overhead. Here are the thunder of truck-loads of coal roaring down the shoots into the wombs of loading steamers, the screams of locomotives, and the clank and creak of steam-cranes. Another plunge, and you are out beyond the station, with the sea beating on the rocks below you and church-yard walls on the cliff overhead.

All this part of Fife is wrinkled and furrowed in ridge and hollow like a chafed sea; it is the shape into which the solid land settled down after the fires that have heaved up the great billow of the Binn and Dunearn Hill ceased to vex it. The main street of Burntisland is in the trough between two of these lower waves of igneous rock, from the crest of one of which Rossend Castle looks down into the harbour, while the other is crowned by the square stolid mass of the Parish Church. Whether the sea ever flowed behind these barriers, making the place an island, let the geologists and the philologists settle among them. This at least is certain, that, under what-ever name it has been known—Wester Kinghorn, Cuningarland, Bertiland—the sea has always been the life-blood of Burntisland, and its port its chief livelihood. Agricola's galleys no doubt came feeling their way round the horn of Rossend when he 'sounded the havens on the north coast of Forth,' Fife being then an unknown land of savages; and the Roman eagles are believed to have taken up their airy station near the crater-lake on Dunearn. And down through the centuries commerce and war have kept an eye on the site. Cromwell took it; and having captured 'great store of great artillery and divers ships,' he found the town 'well-seated, pretty strong, but marvellous capable of further improvement.' It is said that the town, in surrendering, drove a canny bargain, by which the conqueror engaged to solidly pave the streets and repair the harbour, besides fortifying the heights above it; and some of Cromwell's handiwork is extant to this hour.

There are still in Burntisland houses that must have been standing in the Protector's day. The street features of a Fife burgh yield slowly to the influences of time; the old disputes every foot of ground with the new. At the corner of Harbour Place and High Street, the very spot against which the scour and rush of the current of trade bear most strongly, there is a grim-visaged ancient building with a huge roof of grey slate, standing like some hard-grained and stubborn rock in a tide-race, an embodied protest against the spirit

of change.   Long may it stand!   And elsewhere,
not only in the back streets reached by winding

Old House, Burntisland.

lanes and flights of steps, but in the line of the
main thoroughfare, there are well-preserved speci-
mens of the domestic architecture of a former day,

bearing, many of them, the mark of that kindly custom, once much honoured in the Kingdom, by which the spouses inscribed the date and their initials on the front of the dwelling, linking the letters together by a heart, a lozenge, or some craft device, and enclosing them in a moulding or scroll, along with a text of Scripture, or, it might be, an armorial crest, if they had claims of long descent. These speak eloquently of the comfortable well-to-do citizen life, of the family affections, frugal in expression but close-knit and warm, and of the honest burgess pride of the brave days of old.

We stroll through the shady gateway into the grounds of Rossend Castle. This venerable fortalice has known something in the past of war and court doings. Time and man have latterly dealt with it gently. It has caught the art, not bestowed on all men and castles, of growing old gracefully. From its situation, on the ridge between its two seas, it presides over a desirable little territory of its own. On one side the softened clamour of the port and town comes up to it from the foot of the cliff, and the shining waters of the Firth carry the eye across to the forest of ships' masts in Granton and Leith harbours, with Edinburgh Castle and Arthur Seat rising mistily behind. To the north the ground slopes down steeply towards Seamills Bay and its meadows, and then rises to the comb of land opposite, on which are perched the houses of the Kirkton and the fragments of St Adamnan's Church, and behind these to the precipitous sides and wooded scaurs of the Binn, across which, on this day of sun and breeze, shadows are flitting, blurred a little by the smoke from the distillery and the shale works that flank Burntisland's big hill.   The Church of St Adamnan—the successor and biographer of Columba—might of itself furnish forth a chapter. On the site of a Culdee cell, and dedicated by Bishop Bernham in 1243 as the Kirk of 'Litel' or 'Waster Kinghorne,' it has seen history and population flow towards it and away from it ; now it, or rather its surroundings, are again gathering importance.

Old trees are set about the Castle, and on these a colony of rooks are lazily swinging and cawing, and pigeons flutter about the doors.   Ivy mantles warmly the walls of the quadrangular keep, which may date, as the figures near the threshold suggest, from the year 1382   Five hundred years ago, and probably much earlier, it belonged to the Abbey of Dunfermline.   It appears to have been a favourite residence of its Abbots, especially those of the ancient Fife family of Durie of that ilk.   At what period the long western wing was built is apparently not known, but probably it was some time before the Reformation and its conversion to purely secular uses ; the addition on the northern side is obviously of later date.

We were kindly permitted to have the run of the building, from the cavernous kitchen, with its low, vaulted roof and huge fireplace, to the battlements of the tower. It has fallen into good hands, and within as without there has been an endeavour to preserve, as far as possible, the historical features and character of the place. The chief shrine to the pilgrim of romance is Mary Stuart's bedroom, where Chastelard committed his fatal act of folly.

This Room of State is in the first floor of the keep, and, like the adjoining apartments, is wainscoted in old oak. The secret stair that led Chastelard to his doom has recently been come upon in carrying out repairs. It opens out of one of the vaulted rooms below, and conducts, not to either of the oratories or recesses let into the immense thickness of the walls of the State Bed-chamber above, but to a spot near the threshold, where there had evidently been a trap-door. Other hiding places, cunningly concealed by panels, open out of the larger room—the banqueting hall or chamber of dais—behind. The Castle is in truth an ideal place for a game of hide-and-seek. The room assigned by tradition as Cromwell's bed-chamber is on the floor overhead, and is fittingly plain and prosaic. No special *locus* is given to the place of concealment of the relics of Saint Margaret—the skull adorned with jewels and still bearing the 'flowing auburn hair,' which

Abbot Durie had conveyed, first to Edinburgh and then to Burntisland, after the Lords of the Congregation had 'keest doun' their proper shrine. But surely the little oratory in the anteroom with the antique ribbed ceiling, adjoining the drawing-room, were a fit place for their keeping. They drifted to the Jesuit College at Douai, and disappeared in the storm of the French Revolution—perhaps to the Escorial, where they have been 'tint.'

Jeems, the gardener, takes us in tow and instructs us in the Castle's chronology and other matters. 'It 'll be seeven hunner year auld. But I 'll let you see something that was afore 't;' and he points to a couple of cannons that may date from the Great French War. 'No jist sae auld, ye say? Weel, come awa and I 'll show ye the knackiest thing ye ever saw in your lives.' He guides us to the 'Sea-mill,' and explains how the tide, at flow, raises the sluices and fills the great basin behind, and how, with the ebb, the stream finds its way back below the undershot wheel of the flour-mill, until the rising water again chokes it. 'That 's the haill opera,' he muses, peering meditatively down into the gloom, whence rose the skeleton arms of the mill-wheel. 'She broke hersel' a twal'month syne. He 's laid his parks in gress, and there 'll be nae mair grindin' here in God's earth. She 's no goin'; but when she goes she 's a boy!'

Of this nice derangement of genders we meet

Town Hall, West Wemyss.

another example in Burntisland. At the barber's a customer is in front of the mirror, dabbing at a decapitated pimple, seemingly of old standing. 'Ye *hae* planed her doun this time,' he remarks. 'Ay,' responds the discouraged artist with the razor, 'and efter slippin' owre her sae aften!'

The key of the Parish Church is entrusted to us. The building dates from 1592, and is said to be modelled on the old North Church at Amsterdam. It is a monument of the Dutch intercourse and Dutch sympathies of the Burntisland of three centuries back. The building is four-square, with a ponderous outer stair at the eastern side; and the heavy polygonal tower

Burntisland Parish Church.

rising from the centre is supported on massive arches springing from the corners and forming a prominent feature of the interior. Well might Laud, when he came hither on his mission of Anglicising the Scottish service and church furniture, puzzle his brain vainly as to where he should place the altar. Burntisland Kirk was as refractory to priestly guidance from that quarter as were the Burntislanders of the time. The high and mighty prince, King James, renewed within it his oath to uphold the Presbyterian form of worship and government, before the Assembly of 1601 ; and broached the pregnant proposal of an authorised translation of the Bible. The movable 'desks,' fertile source of congregational squabblings ; the votive gifts of ships and the like, hung up in memory of safe and successful voyages to the Baltic or the Arctic Seas, and the 'lofts,' with the mottoes and insignia of the Trades (all except a trace) have been cleared away. But here by the pillar over against the pulpit is the 'seat royal' of the magistrates, in carved oak and gilt, with the date 1606, a present to the church and burgh from its old enemy and provost, Sir Robert Melville.

Near the church door is the tomb of Admiral Fairfax and his wife, parents of Mary Somerville, the astronomer, whose home was on the sea-front opposite the landing-place of the ferry steamers. Dr Chalmers once lived in Craigholm Terrace, and must often have sat by Oliver's Knoll, on the Lammerlaws, or paced the Links or the Long Sands revolving weighty matters of Kirk and State. Such cares we leave closed in behind the churchyard walls. After the example set by Fergusson in his poetical pilgrimage along these 'most unhallowed shores,' we 'regale with sober can,' and, passing out of the High Street into the Links by the East Port and Oliver's cannon,

sunk muzzle downward into the sod, give our
minds for a season to golf.

By the roadside, overlooking the wide stretch
of sands running out at low water as far as the
Black Rocks, is a lean monument. Above it
rises a high, steep cliff, clothed on the warmer
side by fir and birch trees, and patched on its
eastern face by yellow clumps of hardy whin ;
and on the skyline overhead is a sheer wall of
ruddy basalt. It is the 'King's Wud End.'

Six hundred and odd years ago 'Alexander,
our King,' the third of the name, came riding
this way on a dark night. He had dined merrily
in Edinburgh, although it was Lent, and started,
too late for the season and the foul weather,
to join his young queen, married only in the
previous summer, who waited for him in the
Royal Castle of Kinghorn, barely a mile from
this spot. The Lanercost Chronicler tell us that
the master of the King's salt work at Inverkeithing, 'a married man,' using the freedom of the
age, chid him for making a night journey in such
weather and such darkness, and prayed him to
stay the night. But the King laughed, and asked
for guides. He was 'fey,' or 'wud.' His men
and he lost one another, and as he rode round
by the shore, his horse sank its feet in the sand,
stumbled, and threw him ; and 'he bade farewell
to his kingdom.' It was the storm that, according to True Thomas's rede, was to rage from
Ross to Solway—that began the long feud with

England, and put back the hands on the dial
of Scottish history for two centuries. With this
last of our Celtic kings :

> Away wes sonse of ale and brede,
>   Of wyne and wax, of gamyn and glee.

The site of the King's Castle, the dower-house
of the Scottish Queens, seems to have been on
the 'Crying Hill,' the highest part of the Rosslands. This, no doubt, is the *Kin-gorm*, the
'blue headland'—a name corrupted from its old
Celtic form by ignorance and false analogy—that
shelters the snug harbour and sandy bay of
Petticur. The foot-track that runs towards it
athwart the rocky bank, dipping steeply from the
bent-covered braes to the beach, is the 'Wallace
Path,' and may preserve the memory of the
Well-house or Spa, celebrated in a treatise
written in 1618 by the learned Dr Patrick
Anderson, the King's Physician. The water of
this 'Colde Spring'—one or other of the two
little streams that tumble out upon the shore—
when quaffed ' in the morning fasting and at the
rock from which it issues'—was infallible in
'relieving such as are troubled with a difficulty
of breathing, and allaying all inflammations,
internal and external.' Of this tipple should the
inflamed and panting golfer drink, who in vain
urges his ball to mount the hill from the Pump
Hole.

The name of the 'Crying Hill' contains no

allusion to the grief of Queen Yolande. It recalls the already faraway times of the stage-coach and the Ferry Passage. There linger about it echoes of the hoarse shoutings of generations of impatient passengers, eager to cross the Firth to Leith or Newhaven. From the quay-head, and from the shelter of the white-washed walls, many anxious and fearful glances have been cast into the fog and storm outside, and many a limp and bedraggled traveller has crawled from the rocking ferry-boat to dry land.

A solitary smack lies in the tiny harbour of Petticur; it is the craft that carries supplies to the lighthouse-men and garrison of Inch-keith, three miles off shore. That enterprising knight-errant, James the Fourth, once made Inchkeith the scene of a curious experiment to discover the 'original language,' sending thither two infants, boy and girl, to be brought up under the care of a dumb woman. 'Some say,' remarks Pitscottie cautiously, 'they spoke good Hebrew; but as to myself, I know not.' It is an unsolved problem, like Dr Johnson's subsequent proposal to turn this bare and wind-swept isle into a vineyard and fruit garden. Inchkeith has, instead, mounted great guns that command the fairways; and the battery above the columnar cliffs of basalt at Kinghorn Ness keeps companion guard on the Fife shore.

Another twist of the Rosslands Road brings us to the burgh. Kinghorn's main street runs its irregular double rank of tiled and slated houses along the brow of the hill to the Cuinzie Neuk and the Nethergait, where a cataract of old-fashioned dwellings are spilt down the valley of the little stream towards the Church and the boat-harbour, and spread half-way round the margin of the crescent bay. The green 'Braes,' with paths descending to the sands and the rocks, complete the amphitheatre; and here Kinghorn comes to look around it and sniff the caller air when time hangs on its hands. This happens not seldom. For though the old Fife town has always found some work to do, this has, for many generations, been of the casual kind. Its age of royal residence—the memories of Alexander's tristful Queen and of Edward Baliol, who landed here in 1332 ('Clinkhorn,' Galfrid de Baker's Chronicle calls the place), to be defeated by the Earl of Fife, are too faint and far off to trouble it. Kinghorn has made away with its elder antiquities—with the King's Castle on the Ross; the Glamis Tower on the high ground north of the main street; and St Leonard's Chapel in the dell of the burn. But the time when it was the Ferry Town, and was stirred into unwonted life by the coming and going of the passage boats, is still within living memory. There were old inhabitants alive in the 'forties and 'fifties who remembered when the town kept sixty saddle horses for the use of travellers, and when not only were the 'Lion,' the 'Three Crowns,' and the 'New Inn' crowded to the doors, but the whole burgh was turned into a place of entertainment for passengers stayed by tide or storm. And a hundred years ago Kinghorn probably looked back with pride to the classic times sung by Allan Ramsay, when Patie Birnie 'fuffed and peched' over the fiddle he had carried with him to Bothwell Brig and back; and talked with fond regret of high jinks around the old inn table, at which Johnny Stocks the Dwarf assisted by dancing among the punch bowls and claret bottles.

Kinghorn, now that it has closed its spinning-mill, occupies itself a little with shipbuilding, glue, and fishing, but more and more devotes its attention to attracting the golfer and the summer lodger. To this end it has been removing its ancient landmarks. The change, as yet, is visible chiefly around its margin, but is creeping to its centre. Even on the Overgait and the Nethergait an innovating hand is being laid. We miss the old house, with the date 1668, at the head of the steep and winding way, cumbered by forestairs and bait-baskets, which leads from the Town House to the shore. It was once the resi-

dence of Robert Bruce of Falkland, the first
patentee for printing the Bible in Scotland.

Coat of Arms, Kinghorn.

Farther down, under the railway viaduct, is the dwelling
built, as the initials, arms,
and date show, by Treasurer
Henry Schank, in 1638, a
descendant, if legend speaks
true, of that Murdoch Schank
who was the first to come
upon Alexander's body in
1285, and who received for
the service the Castlerig,
which long remained in the possession of the
family and name.

The 'Gang' and the 'Boat Neuk'—the
narrow space between the churchyard wall and
the corner in the rocks where the fishing-craft
shelter—have from time immemorial been the
mart and exchange for the most full-flavoured
of Kinghorn gossip. The shipping and fishing
fraternities were once a stronger power in the
place than they are to-day; and smuggling
was not the least profitable of the burgh industries. The Mariners had their loft in the
plain and ugly cruciform church over the wall,
and at their own charges they erected the
monument to their minister, Maister Thomas
Biggar, who died in 1605 after leading them
'forty years in the desert.' Most of the Kinghorn flock and pastors were staunch to the

Kirk when trial and persecution overtook it.
The talk on the 'Gang' would be worth
hearing in those troublous times — especially
after that Day of Wrath for the Fife shores,
Kilsyth. There were wild women who cursed
the preachers and magistrates that had taken
away their husbands and sons to fight the
Battles of the Lord against Montrose. One,
dealt with by the Session, banned the bailie
as a 'meckle-keited carle,' who had made the
town full of 'faitherless bairns'; and that
rhadamanthine court itself had thin sittings
'from the paucitie of elders, manie of them
being dead and slain at Kilsyth.'

Behind the shipbuilding yard, close to the
railway line and to the footpath that winds
along the shore towards Linktown, is a dingy
building, with courtyard in front and high-
walled garden behind. Its name preserves,
like some half-worn inscription, a record of the
transaction by which the lands of an ancient
Culdee foundation were secularised for the
King's use and converted into an 'Abthanrie.'
To this day the ancient Crown rights are
perpetuated, and were the Sovereign to visit
Kinghorn, 'free lodging' might be claimed in
Abden House. Sorry entertainment would
be found, for this battered old mansion, in
which William Nelson, the publisher, spent his
early years, has been parcelled out among
many poor tenants; the oval shot-holes on

either side of the door and many of the windows have been built up; and the once handsome staircase and the rooms in which (according to local belief; probably it was in an earlier building) Sharp, on his journeys between Edinburgh and St Andrews, was wont to rest and to dine, on 'vyne, flesch, aill, and bread,' have been vilely misused.

The living rock, cropping up at the court-yard entrance, is the same as that trodden aforetime by kings and prelates; but all else has sadly changed. An ancient mariner volunteers his own memories of the place before it was brought so low. With his staff he indicates panels on which, he declares, he has seen the painted shapes of 'prancin' horses and fechtin' men'; they are inch-thick with whitewash and grime. 'An' there's the sub-terrawnean passage'—pointing upwards to a connecting bridge between the first floor and the kitchen wing. He it had been who first came upon the buried jar, containing several thousands of silver coins, hidden between Abden House and the sea. They were of 'King Dauvit's time—saxteen hunner year auld.' This would place the date about mid-way between the Psalmist and the Sair Sanct. In reality the David was David Bruce; the hoard may have been concealed when Edward Baliol and his English made their descent on Kinghorn.

Exhilarating is the coast walk by the East Braes, over turfy bank, rock, and shingle. The rising tide makes flashes and sparkles in the sunlight as it beats on the off-lying Vows Skerries, tumbles in cataracts over the white limestone ledges that project from below the dark overlying masses of trap, and searches its way with many a rebuff and recoil into the crannies of the boulders on the shore. No longer does the seal frequent the ' Bellyfuff' and ' Hochmatoch' rocks, as in the time when the Dunfermline monks claimed a sealgh skin out of every seven taken. But the sea is as wonderful a blue; the salt breeze blows as bracingly.

Beyond the target stands forth, on the water's edge, the lonely shape of Seafield Tower. On this side its walls are breached from base to battlement. Opening on the shore, close by the ledge of red sandstone on which it rises, is a cave, which could tell, among other strange doings, of smuggling exploits, in which the Moultrays of Seafield, before they were 'outed of their fortunes' nearly three centuries ago, did not disdain to bear a hand, in the intervals of feuds with the Kirkcaldys of Grange and other neighbours. Grange-Kirkcaldy is close by; but scarce a vestige remains of the house which was the home of that doughty partisan-soldier who fills so large a place in the story of Mary Stuart's reign, and where the Great

Marquis once came so near being ta'en by his
deadly foes. Kirkcaldys and Moultrays, they
sleep quietly together in Kinghorn kirkyard,
deaf to the voice of the sea and the town talk
on the 'Gang.'

Behoves us to pause a little under the weather-
eaten walls of Seafield before venturing farther.
Scarce a gunshot off begin the bleachfields and
houses of Linktown; and Linktown is Kirkcaldy's knuckle-end.

The 'Lang Toon,' its thin grey line of closely
packed houses over-canopied by smoke, through
which prick here and there a spire or a factory
stalk, stretches away in front behind its sands,
and, as Pathhead and Sinclairtown, climbs the
hill and disappears behind it into space—a town
with a beginning but no end. The parks and
woods of Dunnikier and Raith give it a green
and high background. On one of the nearer
heights, behind Abbotshall Church and the
valley of the Tiel, is Balwearie—the Wizard's
Tower. Sir Michael Scott brought home to
it the forbidden knowledge he had gleaned at
the schools of Padua and Toledo; and on its
battlements the lean old astrologer—does not
his acquaintance Dante, who encountered him
in the Fourth Pouch of the Eighth Circle of
the *Inferno*, call him 'meagre of flank'?—sat
communing with the secret powers of darkness.

He is best remembered around Balwearie and
the Linktown for the trick he played the Devil

who came to claim the recompense of long
service. That must have been a dull-witted
member of the infernal hierarchy who was sent
to cope with the shrewd Fife Faust; for he
undertook as a last labour to twine a rope out
of the sands of Kirkcaldy Bay. Who has
waded, like us, through the dry loose mounds
behind Linktown breakwater, must feel sorry
for the lubber fiend. He laid him down, wearied
of his fruitless toil, and Kirkcaldy, listening
pitifully to his moan 'My taes are cauld!' has
kept adding stone to stone to its length—an
allegory, doubtless, of the triumph of human
will and persistence over the perverse powers
of Nature. 'Some say the Deil's dead and
buried in Kirkcaldy.' Others there are who
stoutly deny it to this day.

Linktown's long thoroughfare is sordid, dingy,
and mean-looking. There is no elbow-room in
its stinted roadway and penurious pavement;
and here and there the corner of a gable pushes
out to the very kerbstone and shoulders the
passenger into the gutter. The inhabitants,
from our sampling, are as frugal of conversation
as of street space. Looking in at a little shop,
we ask the mistress if she can tell us about
the ancient edifice opposite, surmounted by
a half-dismounted belfry. 'Fine that.' 'What
is it, please?'—'A common lodging-house.'
'Well, what *was* it?'—'It's Raith's auld jile';
and we are left to ponder over the sententious

brevity of Fife information. The building was the lock-up of the laird's baron-bailie before territorial jurisdiction came to an end and Linktown was incorporated in Kirkcaldy.

Linktown fits into the 'Lang Toon' proper as the smaller into the thicker end of a telescope. Kirkcaldy itself may have no great reason to boast of the space and beauty of its High Street. But entering it after what we have passed through is like stepping out of one century into a later and brighter. Towards its landward side the town expands cheerfully to the air and sun. It has broad streets, shaded by trees; rows of well-to-do houses surrounded by gardens; and evidences not a few of taste and leisure joined to wealth and trade. Away to the north-west, too, stretching up towards the Raith woods, there is the fine Beveridge Park, where the inhabitants do much disport themselves. But on this lower and older part of the burgh the earlier fashion of building close and treating the sea-breeze as an enemy and intruder still sets its mark. Thus the openings leading to the shore are little better than lanes. One of these wynds is named after Kirkcaldy's most famous son, Adam Smith, the site of whose birthplace, near the foot of the Kirkgait, is now occupied by a bank.

His father was the local Comptroller of Customs. The vicissitudes of fortune of his native port and burgh must have been a familiar tale to him from his youth up. Its progress from the time its ancient possessors the Abbots of Dunfermline, whose 'summer pleasaunce' was at Abbotshall, where Sharp spent his last night on his way to Magus Muir, bestowed on it freedom and burghal privileges; its sufferings in the civil and religious struggles of the seventeenth century; the growth of its maritime trade, until ruin temporarily fell on it with the Treaty of Union; the rise of the Pathhead nailing industry and the Kirkcaldy linen trade— all these were materials lying ready to his hands from which to evolve the laws that make or mar the wealth of nations. A Kirkcaldy legend asserts that Adam Smith, as a child, was stolen by gipsies and carried as far as Kettle. It is curious to speculate what direction the genius that founded modern political economy would have taken had it been diverted to horse-couping and peddling mugs and horn spoons in the fairs and clachans of Fife.

When the Kirkcaldy of an elder day wished to take the air it came forth upon the sands. Here were held many a Covenanting muster, for preaching or fighting. In calmer times, generations of the citizens have waited on the beach for the first sight of the whalers or merchant-ships of the burgh coming in from the great deep, or watched the fleets that had lain wind-bound or becalmed in Leith Roads spreading their sails to the favouring breeze

for the North Sea. Memories of smuggling
days still linger about Kirkcaldy Bay; and the
tale is yet told how, when Paul Jones appeared
in the offing and threatened a descent, that
caustic and pawky clerical humorist, the Rev.
Mr Shirra, knelt down on the sands and prayed
that the Lord would put a hook in the nose
of Behemoth and lead him away backward, and
how accordingly the privateer-men, taking the red
cloaks of the fisherwomen for soldiers assembled
to repel their landing, made haste to sheer off.
The story has also been attached to another
famous Kirkcaldy pastor, Beveridge by name.

Two tall and notable shapes—though neither
of them native to the scene—chiefly haunt Kirkcaldy beach. Thomas Carlyle and 'Tris-
megistus' Irving—both of them young and
with heads and hearts full of things unutterable
—used to pace here in summer twilights, and
watched each long wave as it came rolling to
their feet—'the break of it rushing along
like a mane of foam, beautifully sounding and
advancing, from the West Burn to Kirkcaldy
harbour, the whole mile distance.' Sometimes
these two Annandale lads, the dominies of
rival schools in the burgh, and both of them
in love with the same bright-eyed damsel in
Haddington, would rove the neighbouring woods,
make pedestrian excursions to the caves of
Wemyss, along the coast to Inverkeithing, or
to the summit of the East Lomond, or go on

F.F.   Wemyss Castle.

7

hazardous boat voyages as far as Inchkeith,
returning by moonlight. Afterwards they parted
company and went out into the world, and the
gift of tongues came upon them. But it is
doubtful whether either of them knew a happier
time than he spent in Kirkcaldy. Carlyle speaks
with unwonted geniality of Kirkcaldy society—
'a pleasant, honest kind of fellow-mortals; something of quietly fruitful, of good *old Scotch* in
their works and ways; more vernacular, peace-
able, fixed, and almost genial in their mode of
life, than I had been used to in the Border
homeland.' He had a kindly remembrance of
the fringe of Fife and 'its ancient little burghs
and sea-villages, with their poor little havens,
salt-pans, and weather-beaten bits of Cyclopean
breakwaters and rude innocent machineries.'
It is doubtful whether Kirkcaldy equally appreciated its guests. Irving married a daughter of
the manse; but could make no abiding-place
either in the 'two rooms in a central wynd,'
denominated an Academy, or in Abbotshall
Schoolhouse. As a preacher he had 'owre
muckle gran'ner' for this part of Fife. Afterwards, in June 1828, when he had become the
great pulpit orator of his time, Kirkcaldy
thronged to hear him in the Parish Church.
But it was a day of bitter calamity, for one of
the crowded galleries of the building gave way,
and some thirty persons were killed.

The tower of St Peter's Church, at the head

of the Kirkgait, is Kirkcaldy's chief antiquity. Probably it stands on the site of the original 'Kirk of the Culdees.' It is plain enough in its features, but venerable from the marks of age and hardy struggle with the elements impressed on its grey and massive form.

As we take our seats in the train, the porter passes along from carriage to carriage bawling 'Kirkcawdy!' for the information of travellers. 'Kirkcawdy!' echoes a strident female voice, penetrating through the partition from the next compartment. 'That's whaur Henry Irving used to preach.' 'Henry Irving!' answers another voice of similar *timbre*. 'That would be before he took to the play-actin'.' Then, after a pause, 'I didna ken he was a Stickit Minister.'

KIRKCALDY TO LEVEN.

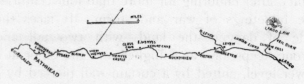

Dysart they call 't; its black and sulphurous caves,
Belch smoke and bellow o'er the neighbouring waves.
George Buchanan.

'IT'S open only on Ne'ar's Day,' is the information given us about Ravensheugh Castle,
after climbing up the hill from Kirkcaldy harbour
to Pathhead. And so we climb down again to
the shore—a far steeper way—through the *heugh*
from which, or from its marrow on the eastern
side of the craggy peninsula, this stronghold of
the lordly line of high St Clair has taken its
name. Seen from the beach below, it looks 'a
protruding shin bone sticking out of the soil of
the dead past'—as strangely bedded and neigh-
boured as the hulk of some antediluvian mammoth
that has been uncovered on the bank of a Siberian
stream. The Kirkcaldy houses press up to it on
one side; and the Dysart woods, just coming
into leaf, nestle against it on the other. Super-
imposed on it is a world whose chief thought and
care is linoleum, and beneath are sunlit sands and
children playing with the waves—'edged with

white,' as when Rosabelle dared them, but gentle and placable at this hour—that wash the toes of the great rock.

Ravensheugh, or Ravenscraig, is remarkably intact, after enduring for more than four centuries the buffetings of war and storm. It faces the side of danger—the land—with two tall and strong keeps, one at a higher and the other at a lower level, united by a curtain-wall pierced by a postern gate, and defended by a moat, which cuts the narrow isthmus uniting it to the high ground on which Pathhead is built. Other defences crown portions of the almost sheer cliff overlooking the sea where attack by escalade was to be feared ; and altogether, as Captain Dugald Dalgetty would say, it is a very pretty piece of military work for its time. James II. of Scots— ' James with the Fiery Face '—formed the design of fortifying this isolated rock ; but it was left to his widow, Mary of Gueldres, to carry out his plan. The castle and lands became, soon after, the compensation given by the Scottish Crown to the St Clairs of Roslin for resigning into the king's hands their independent Princedom of the Orkneys, which had been carried into the family by marriage with Rosabelle, the heiress of the old jarls who held their right from the kings of Norway. Ravenscraig thus commemorates an important incident in the process of welding our islands into one realm.

We make haste to forestall the tide in getting

round the shore rocks towards Dysart. 'Ye'll
hae a gey fecht at the corner,' a baiter had

Ravenscraig Castle.

warned us; and the 'gey fecht' ends in a
retreat to dry land. Here is a pretty bit of
coast fringed by trees, and with spurs of rock

running down into the sea, which has hollowed out long lanes through the softer strata, and paved them with sand up to the grassy lips of the woodland—delectable spots for a quiet bathe.

Dysart comes upon us right suddenly. You dive through a low, dark archway cut in the rock; and lo! you are on the quay between the outer and the inner harbour, the latter an old 'quarry hole,' with trees crowning the perpendicular cliff on one side, and the other blocked in by the walls of weather-beaten old dwelling-houses. In this sheltered dock are crowded a dozen squab and bluff-bowed foreign sailing-craft—Dutchmen and Norwegians most of them—discharging props and cement and loading coal. Beyond their masts and rigging, close down upon the shore, is the tower of the deserted Church of St Serf, ivy-mantled and surmounted by a quaint saddle-backed and crow-stepped gable; and behind it another group of whitewashed walls and red roofs seem to be holding colloquy on the beach and to lean over and peer out into the sea.

Hardly is there room for the strings of coal carts to pass on their dusty way—the Via Carbonaria—between the ruined porch and arches of St Serf's and the retaining wall of the grounds of Dysart House, inside of which, within a stonethrow of the Church, is the cave, now turned into an oratory, where the Saint,

who made Dysart his 'desert,' was so sorely
tempted of Satan.

Clambering up from the harbour shore into
the centre of the burgh, we halt opposite the
Town Hall, whose bell tower might have been

Dysart Harbour.

lifted bodily from some Dutch Rathaus. One
had not to travel farther to learn why Dysart
got its name of 'Little Holland,' or to under-
stand something of the influences which many
centuries of neighbourly intercourse with the
Low Countries have exercised upon the trade
and architecture and customs of this and other

old seaports of Fife. Dysart is a well-preserved
specimen of the little burghs, tenacious of their
ancient traffic and fashions, their faith, and their
municipal privileges that line the northern shore

St Serf's Tower, Dysart.

of Forth, from Culross to the East Neuk. The
'piazzas' have disappeared under which, in
Dysart's best days—say about 1617, when its
Town Hall was built—the merchants and craftsmen of the place met and chaffered with broad-
beamed dealers from Amsterdam or Popperling,

bargaining coal and salt, barrels of beer, and cured fish and hides for cart-wheels and delf-ware, kegs of Holland and pipes of Rhenish; exchanging also views on Church and State affairs, and mayhap congratulations over the latest victory of the 'Protestant Hero' of the Thirty Years' War.

The former 'splendours' of the street life and business movement of Dysart have quite disappeared, save in tradition. But many of the older dwellings retain the antique aspect and strong individuality impressed on them in times earlier than the Union of the Parliaments. There are still rowth of outside stairs and curiously carved corbels, and projections or recesses under winding staircases or behind capacious fireplaces, betraying the 'boleholes,' where many a prize of tobacco, spirits, or silk was stored away from the eyes of the gauger. The old brewhouses, gardens, and cellars, like the caves and clefts by the seashore, might also tell their tales of lawless meetings and of refugees from justice or tyranny, going back to and beyond the time when the 'canty carles of Dysart,' including thirty skippers of the port, fought under the blue blanket of the Covenant, until, on the field of Kilsyth, they were 'a' wede away.'

Casting a backward glance at Dysart and its memories as we follow the shore by the 'Piper's Braes' towards the Red Rocks, and

leap the cataract of reeking hot water that
tumbles down to the beach from the colliery
works above, it seems to us that there has always
been about it a sniff of sulphur—a reminder of
the thin partition between it and the fires of
Tophet. Is it not preserved in the local nomenclature; for instance in the 'Hell Pot Wynd,'
which recalls one of the many occasions on which
the coal seams have caught fire and burned with
a fierceness and dourness like that with which the
Fife folks of old flung themselves into any work,
good or evil? By this way Michael Scott may
have come to keep tryst with his neighbour, the
Laird of the Wemyss, concerning the defence
of the Kingdom and the bringing back of the
'Maiden of Norway,' who, to Scotland's dule,
died, from the rough handling of the North Sea,
on reaching the Orkneys. At these fantastic red
crags at Blair Point, the Witches of the Wemyss
met at midnight and worked their spells for
raising the wind; at least here the godly made
a bonfire of them for the encouragement of
others. The Vicar of Dysart is believed to have
hunted and caught the aged Walter Myln, the
last of the Protestant martyrs, on the Piper's
Braes; and this rough beach was the skirmishing
ground between the French troops, landed at the
harbour by Mary of Guise, and the Lords of the
Congregation, whose men 'laye in their claithes,
their boits never aff,' for three weeks, 'skirmishing almost every daye, yea sum dayes even from

morne to nicht.' And later, when the quarrel
ran as hot, or hotter, between Presbyter and
Prelatic, the recalcitrant Synod of Fife, locked
out of St Serf's Church by order of James VI.,
met by the seashore and carried on their polemic
for two hours 'in spite of drenching rain and the
King's authority'; and Oliver's panic-stricken
troopers no doubt fled thither when a thunderbolt
struck the Town Hall in which they were lodged.

In a niche of the Red Rocks a local weaver
of forty years since has hewn a memorial of
himself, in the shape of a figure, in relief, of
the 'Prisoner of Chillon,' chained to a huge ring
and staple in his dungeon wall and raising
clasped hands in agonised appeal against his
fate—a work of patience rather than of art.
West Wemyss—a little group of masts and
chimneys—now peeps at us round its corners
and through its smoke. The 'Lock-out Road'
bends gently round towards it, following the
curve of the shore and of the wooded hills
behind. These are turning to purple and green
under the breath of spring. The spring colours
are everywhere—green on the grass and trees;
white, like snow, sprinkled on the spikes of the
blackthorn or heaped in drifts on the branches
of the wild cherry-trees; yellow on the bunting's
breast, the willow catkins, and the primroses
edging the path.

The land here and now is as fresh and glad-
some as the sea; and we have to leave it to

plunge into stour and racket and evil smells.
But first there is a pretty peep, at the Chapel
Garden, of a white cottage and a trim pleasance
enclosing a fragment of grey ruin of half ecclesiastical, half manorial aspect, with a wonderfully
weather-eaten gable-end turned towards the sea
—an ancient church which has somehow lost its
history, at least in local memory.

While we stop to take into our minds and
notebooks this picturesque approach to West

West Wemyss.

Wemyss—the lofty cliffs veined with piping, the
brick stalks rising through the trees, the colliery
gangways and workings below, the little harbour
at the point, and beyond it the perspective of
the village street, closed by the quaint, lean,
narrow-windowed steeple of the Town House—
a faint boom sounds across the water, and a
group of grimy pitmen turn round to tell us
that it is the Edinburgh gun. 'Do you know
Barncraig?' we venture to ask. But they all
shake their heads. 'It's the auld pit; it was
closed lang before oor time.'

They can tell us plenty about the pits still

at work and discharging their laden trucks into daylight upon the crowded harbour pier. Past these we must pick our way along narrow platforms, among tramway rails and points, with crags and pithead machinery overhead, and the thud of the engines mingling with the plash of the waves against the wooden piles underneath.

Few of the inhabitants of the dingy little barony burgh are about as we saunter through its single street. Town and townsfolk look commonplace and woebegone to the casual eye. The lean Dutch steeple invading the thoroughfare, and squinting suspiciously up and down the street through the narrow slits of windows set under a penthouse of zinc, seems the one outstanding object in the place. Houses and people wear in their faces that peppery grey look which the 'Chronicles of Barncraig' tells us comes from an impregnation of coal dust. After all, how little the passer-by can guess of the volumes of human history, both tragedy and comedy, hidden behind the surface he sees! They are to be read only by one who sits down and patiently studies them, and who brings to the task something of the poet's sympathy and power of divination. Thus, while we tentatively identify the 'Cox'l' and the 'Poun's,' the Windy Wynd, the How Head and the Hine, and fancy we catch a glimpse of Sandie Fernie's mahogany-tinted

features near the harbour, there are none of
the faces peering through the panes that can
be taken for those of the Linty or Cobbler
Swankey, and no figure near the well or the
store door that fits the story of Auld Ailie.

Out again upon an iron shore, where, below
high-water mark, beside weed-draped rocks
and barnacled fragments of wreck, there gushes
up through the stones a strong stream of fresh
water—like a spring of happy memories among
dead hopes. Wemyss Castle is on the wooded
cliff overhead. It thrusts its plain white
western wing through its trees, and flaunts its
flag against the blue sky. Its roots are in
the rock-hewn chapel, passages and 'bottle
dungeon' underneath. As we move round
opposite the front and the older eastern flank
of the Castle, its aspect changes. It becomes
imposing and stately—a lordly 'Castle by the
Sea,' that has the history of good and evil
times plainly written on its strong and frowning walls, its corbelled turrets, and machicolated
string-courses. Macduff was the earliest recorded 'Lord of the Caves,' and its later
owners claim to be his descendants. Here
might have been the hold of the Thane of
Fife, although there are many rival sites near
us—a 'Macduff's Castle,' only a mile to the
eastward; another, at Kennoway, two or three
miles inland. At least there has been a
Wemyss of Wemyss for six hundred years

and more. For witness, is there not the
silver basin, given as a drinking bowl by
Eric of Norway to the 'noble Scot' who came
to convey home the King's daughter, and now
turned to the pious use of a family baptismal
font?

No emissary of the Psychical Research
Society has yet questioned 'Green Jean,' the
unquiet spirit that is said to flit through the
darkling Castle chambers, and extracted from
her her forgotten story. But the tale of
Mary Stuart's first meeting here with her
young cousin Darnley is well remembered, and,
to us that know its context, is sadder and
stranger than any ghost legend. The Queen
was light of heart, hunting, hawking, and in
the evening dancing, when her cousin Darnley,
a proper young man and tall, came riding
thither out of England. The 'lang lad,'
who, as Melvill tells us, was 'even and brent
up, weill instructed in his youth in all honest
and comely exercises,' took his sovereign's eye
when she met him in the presence chamber,
now reduced to the steward's room, opening
from the old court. There were great feastings
at Wemyss, then in the hands of the Queen's
half-brother, Moray; and the Caleb Balder-
stones of the lairds and lords of Fife, who
entertained the royal train on their progress,
long remembered their visits, for 'there was
such superfluity of banqueting as was never

seen before within this realm, which caused the wild fowl to be so dear that partridges were sold at a crown apiece.' The woods and the green links by the shore might tell of softer passages in that time of short-lived hope, when love was young and Darnley kind. The 'lang lad' carried all his good qualities on his outside; and the match so hastily made was repented all too soon.

Tradition says that Mary could wield a golf club as well as fly a hawk and foot a measure, but it does not add that she played a match with her young kinsman and suitor over the Wemyss Castle links. Like her father, James V., when he was in peril with the gipsies in one of the caves near by, or like her great grandson, Charles II., who paid two flying visits, as an exiled prince, to Wemyss, she had other things to distract her mind. Yet all three might have found type and warning of their own fortunes in this errant and adventurous course. It is full of surprises and misfortunes for the rash and un-wary. Narrow and besprent with hazards is the territory between the impending hill and that grave of hopes, the shore; and you may play over a pinnacle of red rock and 'hole out' at the mouth of a cavern. We, too, like Dogberry and the Royal Stuarts, have our losses. Only one instance do we know of a visitor to the links of Wemyss who never lost

The May—from the Sphinx Rock, St Monans.

a ball. It is that of a friend who trained his
dog to hunt the dodging gutta downwind.

The nearest and grandest of the Wemyss
Caves opens its hospitable portals to receive
us. Three stupendous archways face east, west,
and south, like the fragment of some cyclopean
cloister; and, within, the roof rises dome-wise
to a height of a hundred feet, and has been
pierced by a shaft. This is the 'Glasswork
Cave'; and in it may be said to have begun
that manufacture of bottle and window glass
in which Scotland strove, but long in vain, to
rival the work of the French craftsmen driven
over to the neighbouring kingdom by the
revocation of the Edict of Nantes. Ages
before, this and the other Wemyss caves must
have been the homes of troglodyte natives of
the Fife shores, who have left their strange
Pictish symbols and figures of man and beast
sculptured high on the walls—a lettering that
gives only dubious answers to the questions
of the archæologist.

We are not so lucky as a visitor to this
cave a generation ago, who found 'under its
cool shade the cows of the two neighbouring
villages assembled; by and by the village
maidens came to milk them. Here and there
long lines of sunbeams, bursting into the gloom
through the lofty archways, lighted up a
singular scene of beauty.' But although we
miss the cows and the village maidens, there

are the shafts of sunlight, barring the shadows of the cave, and, without, the vivid green of the meadows, the vivid red of the rocks, the pale-blue sky, and the turquoise-blue sea.

East Wemyss is a snug, cleanly, white-washed village, with orchard-trees well sprinkled among the houses, rising woods and fields behind it, and a fine rocky shore in front. It looks a delightful place for a quiet holiday —for a little golf, a little bathing, perhaps a little sketching, and a great deal of restful enjoyment of the changeful charms of sea and shore. We would fain linger and know more thoroughly this Sleepy Hollow, but must not. An ancient doocot, picturesquely perched on the spur of coast, points our eastward way. Behind it is a beautifully situated cemetery climbing a hill and descending a dell to the sea, a strange contrast to some of the old churchyards we have passed. Below it is a spacious cave, through the two doorways of which this wonderful shore-walk is threaded. It is the Court Cave, where the courts of barony were held in elder times—where the Guidman of Ballangeich found lodging with the gipsies. Macbeth's Hold—its twin towers battered out of shape by time, which has left it a name but no history to speak of—surmounts the cliff in front, and beneath it, fringing a new stretch of links, are more caves. These also have their uncouth tracings

of shapes of snake, mammoth, and dragon;
cross, circle, and horse-shoe; their paved
floors; their seats hewn in the living rock

Court Cave, Wemyss.

But the entrances are low; and the interiors
—even that of the capacious Doo Cave, which
is lighted from the pigeon-holes high up the
cliff—are dark and noisome.

Who would potter and peer in a hole in the
earth, with the sun-glint on the links and a
making tide creaming the tawny curve of Buckhaven Bay? The ribs of many a gallant boat
protrude from these sands. It is a cemetery of
wrecked and worn-out fishing craft, as full of
memories for the sunburned toilers of the sea
who live on the cliff above as is the churchyard itself. A crooked way leads down to the
harbour at the point, where a few grizzled salts
are seated on fish-boxes and piles of spars
watching a crew hoisting with musical cries
their brown-tanned sail to a freshening wind
outside the bar. On the high ground in rear
there is the semblance of a street. But elsewhere there is no more order about the Buckhyne houses than about seabirds' nests on
a shore cliff. They cling to the rock like
barnacles. To follow the coast is to wind in
and out among narrow passages, terraces, and
flights of steps, all rendering upon the salt
water which runs up between the long reefs
under the doors and windows of the fisherfolk.

Everywhere you turn the way is encumbered
by creels and lobster-baskets and coils of
baited lines—the outlook blocked by festoons of
brown, white-lettered bladders. Oilskins and
sou'westers and drying fish hang on both sides
of the lintels ; and on the steps are sonsy
fisherwomen shelling clams, baiting lines, and
mending nets.

A wild spot this in a south-easterly gale! Small wonder if the faces of the Buckhaven folk be constantly turned seaward, and if their thoughts and talk be pickled in ocean brine. The sea is their familiar neighbour, their great benefactor, their ruthless enemy. Its changeful voice is the undertone of their whole lives— their lullaby and their dirge. They are a peculiar people, the descendants, it is said, of a colony of Brabanters who settled during Alva's persecution on this western horn of Largo Bay. A douce and sober folk they look, in their sad-coloured raiment. But no more bold and skilful fishers lie at the lines on the North Sea or follow the Herring Draive round the coast. Surnames are as frugally distributed among them as are ideas; and when you have mentioned the Thomsons and Robertsons you have well-nigh exhausted the village. According to fisher custom, identification is helped out by 'tee' or 'slug' names. But they must be cautiously used. Once, says a Buckhaven legend, two fishermen met at the brae-head and exchanged a friendly weather greeting. 'Windy, Willie!' said one. 'Terrible, Tammy!' replied the other. Inadvertently each had spoken his neighbour's nickname, and they fell on one another tooth and nail.

'Sawney, Jock, and Janetty' are much in evidence on the stairs and at the nooks of the lanes. Indeed, we have heard Buckhyne tersely

summed up as 'Shells, smells, and bairns.'
These last, like Fife bairns in general, are not
blate. One sturdy urchin brusquely accosts the
artist while he is washing in a bit in water-
colour with the sands as foreground—'Will ye
pent my boat?' 'Bring it here then, laddie,'
says the sketcher good-naturedly, thinking of
toy craft. 'She's doon in the hyne; I'll sune
row her roun',' is the prompt response. Such
is the lear gotten in Buckhaven College.

Methil is the neighbour of Buckhaven to
the east. Prosperity has come to it from time
to time like a tidal wave, and left it again
stranded high and dry. But yesterday it was
a deserted and tumble-down village, living on
the memory of the days before its upsetting
neighbour Leven had been heard of, when it
was a busy and thriving place, with salt-pans
and windmills and a shipping trade. To-day
it is again at the top of the flow. It is
the chief port of shipment of the Fife coalfield.
Large steamers come into its capacious docks
and load under the great coal shoots; acres
of ground are covered with railway sidings and
stores; and houses sprout up like mushrooms.

Alas, for the mellow impasto which time had
begun to spread over Old Methil! A black
smear is over it all. Coal-bings are heaped
high on the classical links of Dubbieside, on
which great feats were done by the ancient
champions of golf. There is still a strip of

turf set aside for the game on the slope of the
Kinarchie Braes. But the glory has long fled
across the Leven and the Scoonie Burn.
Before even coal-dust and sand-drift had laid
waste the scene, the better had proved the
enemy of the good—Lundin had vanquished
Dubbieside.

Methil's ghost—Thrummy Cap—has likewise
deserted the scene. It was the spirit of a
Dutch wood-contractor who failed during his
lifetime in his efforts to get his account squared
with the laird. So, with a dogged persistency
worthy of Vanderdecken himself, he came back
from the dead to present again and again his
little bill. There may be a statute of limita-
tions to such debts in the spirit-world. But it
is more probable that the poor spook, disturbed
by the unwonted clatter and stir, has *forhooeyed*
the old red house, shaped like a two-decker,
that stands at the harbour end.

Dubbieside scorns its homely name, and calls
itself Innerleven. You may listen in vain for
the click of the weaver's shuttle as you take
your way through the dingy main street that
leads to the waterside. As well look for the
silver scales of the salmon in the stream that
flows hither, laden with the scum of bleachfields and paper - mills, from Loch Leven.
Salmon and hand-loom weaving belong, like
the Danes who fought their battles on Leven
banks, to the unrestorable past. Leven town,

a pleasant modern fact, makes a brave show from the opposite bank. Its harbour is silted up; a port of refuge for waterlogged fishing-boats, towed here out of the strife of winds and waves, to end their days in calm waters and sink and drown decently in their own element.

Happily Leven is not dependent on its trade. It has a mine of wealth in its links and sands. Its fortune is in the fresh breezes that play upon its bent hills and in the lovely sweep of Largo Bay, reaching in towards the base of the smooth green Law and stretching away to where the headland of Kincraig Point fronts the white cliffs of the Bass. When, in the Golden Age of Golf, a village wakens up to find itself planted on the skirts of a playground like Leven Links, it may wash its hands of coal and ochre and other sordid business stains, and cheerfully devote itself to ministering to the pleasure and healthful exercise of its guests and frequenters. Its past history, if it has any, it can afford to forget; in the present there is enough to satisfy the soul of every reasonable man. And so it comes that few of the residents of Leven, and scarce any of its visitors, could pass an examination in the troublous kirk history of Scoonie Parish; that the Town Cross —the fragments recovered from an old wall and put together behind an institute—is passed by with an idle glance; and that the multitudes who disport themselves on the sands neither know nor care to know that Charles II. came hither from Wemyss in holiday humour to 'ride at the glove' before setting out on a vainer errand for Worcester.

As we move eastward, the close-built streets that converge on the harbour fray out into lines of pleasant villas and cottages, flanked and backed by gardens. The human heart also expands to the genial influences of the air and sun ; and before we reach the teeing-ground the spirit of Golf enters and takes possession. By the Scoonie Burn—the yellow Pactolus of these Elysian Fields—wanders their guardian genius, 'Robert,' and to his mild challenge : 'Ye 'll hae a ticket, nae doot?' the conventional tribute must be paid before one may pass over and follow the gutta ball in its devious and adventurous flight. In the billowy folds of this Enchanted Ground lurk calamity and disappointment—bunkers where the timid and the rash are alike entrapped, evil 'lies' and scrapes that turn confidence into despair, and dread places, such as the Stygian stream of pit-water that is moat to the rampart of the Mile Dyke, or that meandering Cocytus beyond—'Piggy's Burn'—above which curses muttered over lost balls and bungled shots seem to hover perpetually,

This is a region thick set with gins and traps and snares—a place where surprise,

mischance, and mysterious disappearance have
happed immemorially.   One remembers that
three centuries ago a laird of Leven Links—
that great lawyer and collector of Decisions,
Gibson of Durie—was caught up bodily by a
band of mosstroopers while taking his exercise
on the fringes of Fife, and buried for weeks
from human ken in a Border peel tower until
a law plea had been decided in his absence.
This was worse even than 'tynin' a ba'.'

At length that bane of golfers, the railway line,
draws to the sea, or the shore bends towards the
railway, and in front the bent hills rise impending.   The half-course is finished, and we climb
a green barrier to find the Firth dimpling and
sparkling at our feet.   Here one can rest and
draw pure, full draughts of life.   Surely nowhere
does the water have so marvellous a play of
colour, or break in such showers of light on rock
and sand.   While a red-coated golfer turns his
face westward, shading his eyes with his hand
against the level sun, lest peradventure his ball
go astray and be lost in sandy places, our gaze
is out to sea, where a fisher boat is steering for
home.   There also is our haven of rest, and we
make for it over tussocky sand-hills which the
truant feet of Alexander Selkirk must have
known full well, long before they paced sentry
on the desolate rock of the South Sea.   Smooth
is the path of the waters ; the brown sail is
lowered off Lundie Ledge, and the boatie rows

in before us, and, while we are still steering through the scattered cottages of Drumochy, is moored already by the little pier. A handful of houses cluster at the foot of the hill, the biggest of them giving bield from the east wind to the tiny harbour. A glen opens into the land, and over it, and over houses and fishing-boats, straddles an ugly railway viaduct. Farther back it curves in green folds; glints of red roofs against a background of wood tell the whereabouts of the Kirkton and Lundin Mill; and over all is the cloven head of the Law.

This is Lower Largo.

LARGO TO ELIE.

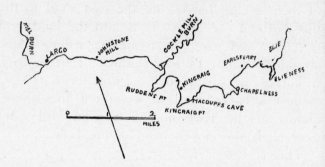

I cuist my lines in Largo Bay.—*The Boatie Rows.*

WE cast our lines by Largo Bay ; and they fall on pleasant places. Says the brisk old Fife stave :

> Up wi' the canty carles o' Dysart,
>   And the merry lads o' Buckhaven,
> And the saucy limmers o' Largo,
>   And the bonnie lasses o' Leven.
>   Hey ! ca' thro', ca' thro' !
>   For we hae mickle ado.

And mickle ado have we to tear ourselves from moorings, and ca' thro' a stage which is to bring us to Elie or Pittenweem. For when limmers o' Largo wile you to the Ladies Links, to the gaunt shapes of the Three Stones that stand near the ruined Tower of Lundin like withered beldames turned to rock while about some deed without a name, or to the moss-fringed well of Lundin Mill, where the patriarch of trout no longer lurks, time speeds, ah, too quickly! Or you may be enticed from the forthright track to follow the shady mazes of the Serpentine Walk, and this will bring you past the lodge of Largo House, to the hamlet, the hospital, and the kirk of Upper Largo—the 'Kirkton'—seated on the knees of the Law. In an older Largo House, of which a fragment is still standing, dwelt that stout and bold sailor, Sir Andrew Wood, when his last sea-fight had been fought, and his ships, the *Mayflower* and the *Yellow Caravel*, no longer needed to cruise the Forth, keeping a keen look-out for Stephen Bull and the English pirates rounding the Bass. Traces are yet to be seen of the canal which the old sea-dog caused to be dug, that he might be rowed in state to church in his eight-oared barge. It was a later laird of Largo—one of the Durhams—who, according to Mr Wood's *East Neuk of Fife*, first christened Edinburgh 'Auld Reekie,' and timed his household prayers by its rising smoke—'It's time, bairns, to tak' the buiks, and gang to bed; for yonder's Auld Reekie puttin' on her nichtcap.'

You may even be drawn on to explore the depths of Kiel's Den, and there, belike, glimpse some ghost of the past flitting through the greenwood. It may be that forgotten Viking—the Tammie Norrie of local folklore—who sleeps under the mound of Norrie's Law, and whose sword and *byrnie* of silver mail were pilfered from him by some ferreting cadger. Or that bluff and faithful Lord Lindsay, owner once of the battered crow's nest of Pitcruvie Castle, who stood up and to his face reproved James the Fourth for his unfilial conduct at Sauchie. It is still more like to be the wandering spook of Largo's 'Robinson Crusoe.' Fortune drifted him back and cast him ashore at his native village. But he found that even Largo society irked him, and stole away to Kiel's Den to hunt for that spirit of solitude that had been his familiar in the rocky recesses of Juan Fernandez.

Down by the harbour and the shore one has a yet better chance of forgathering with memories of Alexander Selkirk. The full tide laps gently against the pier, the traditional mart of business and exchange of news of the village. The sea, a good familiar creature, plays round the bases of the old warehouse, now the snug 'Crusoe Inn,' and the other houses by the water's edge, and croons softly the eerie song that fills those who listen to it with the mad passion for wandering. Here—

> Among the waste and lumber of the shore,
> Hard coils of cordage, swarthy fishing-nets,
> Anchors of rusty fluke and boats up-drawn—

Selkirk spent his days as a youngster. And here, after he had sailed with Dampier and seen many strange lands and faces, he sat with his cronies and told over again that wondrous

Ancient Mariner's tale that on his way home he
had poured into the ears of Defoe, who had
stumbled on him at Wapping. Perhaps he was
little better than a returned beachcomber and
ne'er-do-weel. Boy and man he was very

Largo Harbour.

different from the exemplary hero of the Sunday
School prize-book. In his youth he had 'thrawed
his mouth' at the minister, and was in the
Session's black-books, and a South Sea training
in the beginning of the eighteenth century was
not the choicest moral discipline. But much
more than was ever laid to the charge of
Alexander Selkirk will be forgiven to the

marooned Largo sailor whose story inspired the
great latter-day legend of the English-speaking
race, and has kindled in the breasts of generations of lads the love of manly adventure, and
strengthened in them the will 'to strive, to
seek, to find, and not to yield.' One likes him
for coming back to the old village at the mouth
of the Kiel Burn, and for buying the old house
that his father might end his days in it in
comfort. It has been removed—more's the
pity!—and his great sea-chest and musket and
cocoa-nut drinking-vessel have drifted elsewhere.
But an inscription on a new building on the left-
hand side of the road, as you go through the
part of the village lying east of the burn—known
of yore as the 'Temple of Strathairly'—marks
the place; and in front of it is a statue of the
unshorn and stalwart castaway—'the shipwrecked
sailor waiting for a sail'—clad in goat-skins, and
peering out to sea under his hollowed palm for
sight of the long-delayed rescue.

In vain; for Largo has been discovered by
the wandering race of summer visitors, and
their many-storied caravanserais begin to block
out Crusoe's birthplace from the shore. Already
the tawny beach is strewn with sprawling
youngsters, busy, at this hour of high tide,
investing the positions of their nurses and
guardians with moat and fortification, or launch-
ing their frail craft on a benign sea that meets
the land with barely a ripple, and only hints,

F.F.

The Neuk, St Monan's.

9

by a timber sticking up through the loose sand, of its angry and hungry moods.

The village is behind us ; and we tread 'the bent sae brown.' Nowhere by the shores of Fife, unless it be in the wilds of Tent's Moor, is there so desert and solitary a place as this waste, known of old as Drumeldrie Links, that borders the eastern recesses of Largo Bay. It is a wild given over to windlestrae and thistle, with here and there a boulder, dropped on the flat and sandy sea-floor far back in the Ice Age. A firm and springy pathway wanders among the round-headed hillocks of blown sand, thinly thatched by the bleached and dishevelled bent ; and in the sunnier spots are blotches of purple thyme and the tiny yellow stars of the tormentil. The creaking cry and plunging flight of the peewit seem to haunt this empty place. But if you lift up your voice and shout, a great flock of gulls will rise and circle round towards the sea, and scores of rabbits will scurry into their holes ; or perhaps a velvet-coated mole will start up at your foot and begin digging a cave of refuge in the loose earth for dear life.

And so we come to where the Cocklemill Burn meanders through the sandy solitude, exposing high banks, honeycombed with martins' nests, and losing itself in a tidal marsh between us and the long spur of Ruddon Ness. To wade or to jump is a dread alternative for such as have been endowed by nature with short

legs. We drag a floundering figure from the
slough of despond, and wipe the Cocklemill mud
from its nether limbs before wending onward,
round the beautiful white crescent of Shell
Bay, and up the narrow pathway, between the
cultivated land and the sea cliffs, to the summit
of Kincraig Head.

In clear weather the head of Kincraig Braes
must be a glorious vantage-ground for surveying
Fife and the coasts thereof. The precipices of
black trap and basalt drop almost sheer into
the sea, sixty or seventy yards below, and at
their feet are strewn sharp and jagged fragments
of rock like rows of shark's teeth. A terrible
turmoil must be here when the wind blows hard
out of the south-east, and the waters are lashed
against these frowning bastions. To-day you
can look down into their clear, calm, green
depths. But a moist breath from the North
Sea has begun to fill the Firth, and through
it, looking seaward, you can barely discern the
Bass and Berwick Law looming up like a
pair of huge and spectral pyramids.

On the land side the ground slopes smoothly
down to the bed of the burn, and then rises
again to the high ridge which, near at hand, is
flanked to left and right by the heights of
Largo Law and Kellie Law. Close beside us,
on the brae-face, is the substantial old house of
Kincraig, with its dilapidated doocot—a manor,
now turned into a farm-house, which has been

in the possession of the Gourlays since the days of William the Lion. The gaunt walls and chimneys of the burned Grange are also near at hand. By it passes the ancient 'Cadger's Road,' from the landing-place of the Earl's Ferry, where so many have stepped ashore since St Cuthbert's time to pass on and make history in Fife. The Earl of Mar was one of these; and the Jacobite lairds of the Kingdom convened in the house of Malcolm of Grange to hatch the rebellion of '15. The old road ascends by Muircambus and Balchrystie, making its way, by Kiel's Den, towards Falkland. It, and a branch route over the crest of the ridge by Rires, can be traced past many a spot famous in history and romance. The fine tower of Kilconquhar Church rises above the trees that screen the village and loch; it was an heiress of Kilconquhar —'Kinneuchar' in every

Kilconquhar Church.

Fife ear—that the Bruce made his bride. Balcarres Craig and Balcarres House, the home of the Lindsays, whose family history is one long chapter of romance, are fair in sight. In the herd's cottage on the hill behind lived 'Auld

Robin Gray,' and the song that has drawn so many tears was written by a blythe daughter of the Licht Lindsays, sitting at the little turret window facing Kincraig and the sea.

Then, overlooking the Craig itself, is the site of the Castle of Rires; and there, if ever there was a Macduff (which historians doubt), dwelt the Thane of Fife. One must not doubt while seated on Kincraig Braes. For in the face of the rock below is not the worn remains to be seen of the cave where he found shelter from the usurper? And while his wife held politic parley at his *rath*, three or four miles away on the ridge above, with Macbeth, did he not take flight from Earlsferry; and did he not in gratitude confer on that ancient burgh a share of those 'privileges of Clan Macduff,' which he had asked of his rightful king when he had brought him to his own, namely, that no boat should be put off from shore in pursuit of a fleeing homicide until the escaping sail was half-way across the Firth?

Elie Links sweeps round the back of the town and comes down to the sea-margin between Earlsferry Point and the foot of the bluff of Kincraig. The putting-greens, from our height, show on it like tiny little discs of lighter verdure on which mannikins are going through mystic evolutions. Nor, when we have come down 'by the run' to the plane on which they move, do they seem less intent on their game. Your golfer of the earnest type would not allow himself to be put off his game although Behemoth were to bellow at him from behind the rocks of Coalbaikie.

On the Chapel Ness or Point of Earlsferry there is another green and quiet spot for meditation. Between us and the huge old granary on Elie Ness the sandy bay curves like a sickle, and behind it in a continuous line—for the two little burghs have grown into one—is the cheerful and thriving-looking sea-front of Elie and Earlsferry. Fashion has discovered the place ; but at no time does it surge tumultuously around this bold green headland, set apart, 'of old past the memory of man,' to the solace of weary and storm-tossed travellers. The foundations of the ancient chapel, attached to the Hospital which stood here under the pious care of the Nuns of North Berwick, are still above ground, and behind the eastern gable wall shelter is to be found when the winds buffet the Ness too rudely.

Embarkings and disembarkings many have been witnessed from the Chapel Ness since Macduff was ferried hence to the 'land beyond the sea.' Off the Vows beacon King David Bruce and Margaret Logie were in such dire distress of shipwreck that they vowed to build a church to St Monan as the price of safety. At least so runs the story, although 'Vows,' or 'Voos,' —we have met with the name before on the Fife

coast—has probably another and older derivation.
From hence, too, the Duke of York's coxswain
stole away with the Belle of Elie 'coopered up in
a barrel with a head of open spars'; and 'Old
Borlum' and his Highlanders of the '15, after
nailing to a tree the ear of the Laird of Elie's
groom, as a 'sour Whig,' slipped by night
through the line of watchful frigates to land at
Jova's Neuk, under the brow of Gullane Hill
opposite, and make their bold dash at Edinburgh.
'The Elie' was always a haven of refuge; but
perhaps none ever appreciated its welcome and
shelter more than good Master James Melville,
minister of Kilrenny and nephew of Andrew, the
Boanerges of the Reformation, who sets down in
his 'Diary,' under the year 1580, the particulars of
the 'maist pitiful and lamentable' voyage he made
thither from North Berwick in 'a mickle coal
boat.' For shipping unadvisedly, with 'but ane
auld man and twa young boys,' and as passengers
'a boy, the nurse, and an Englishwoman, a
soldier's wife in Berwick wha had a desire to come
with the bairn into Scotland,' the 'little pirrhe of
east wind' with which they set out died away,
and night came down on a tumbling and yawing
boat and a sick boat's company, until 'at last the
Lord looked mercifully on, and sent, about the
sun going to, a thick haar from the south-east,
sae that getting on the sail that was upon her,
within an hour an a half, nae wind blowing, we
arrivit at the Ailie; and after a maist wearisome

and sair day, gat a comfortable night's lodging
with a godly ladie at Carmury.'

Earlsferry and Elie folks are never left to
sigh long in vain for a 'pirrhe of wind' from
the east or some other quarter. The air and
the sea around them are in constant motion.
The waves seem to dance more buoyantly
than elsewhere about the Vows Rocks and the
Heads. The sands of the bay are a very
playground for the breezes. Between the
common and the sea the clean and handsome
houses are sprinkled—a long but thin array.
There is plenty of space for the briny, fragrant
breath from the open mouth of the Forth, or
the gentler airs from landward, to sift freely
through from beach to links and links to
beach, and keep the streets constantly sweet
and fresh. And from the grass to the sands
and back again move the frequenters of the
place, as suits the hour or the weather, the
whim of the moment or the will of the wind.
They do but frugally use the little main street
of Earlsferry that meanders through the burgh,
for half of the time under orchard walls and
overhung by trees.

But, quiet as is this western end of Elie
Bay, the aroma of the past has almost all
exhaled from it. The eye does not fall upon
a house that would fitly lodge a fugitive
homicide or smuggler or a roystering royalist
of other days; such tenants would take ill

with the presence of the summer visitors. The excellent historian of the 'East Neuk,' of whom the red-steepled United Free Kirk further east is a conspicuous memorial, was able to recover a hazy reminiscence of the old-fashioned look of the 'Torret House,' and of a bed, with satin hangings, 'apple-green, and a darker shade of the same colour,' which, legend had it, was that slept in by the Duke of York when he was wont to cross over from Leith to 'The Elie' to solace himself with golf and the company of the Fife lairds, before fate had called him south to be the last of the Stuart Kings.

These were among the last scraps of old romance that clung to the twin burghs. The tide of change has taken them with it and drifted them into the front of the fashion among Fife watering-places. In Sibbald's time the elder of them was a 'little fisher town.' It had washed its hands of fish before stretching them out to join those of its younger and more enterprising neighbour, Elie. Beside that spruce and well-busked place Earlsferry still wears a sedate, elderly-sister air. But it is old-fashioned only by comparison. The few remaining cottages of earlier date are being elbowed into the background; spick and span new villas thrust in between them and the roadway. A remnant of the Fife dwelling-houses of the elder type have closed their ranks and rallied around the ancient Town House steeple. But even these confess, by the bugging out of a bow-window or the cutting away of a forestair, that although they may have a foot in the past they have an eye on the present. The steeple itself has been redd up, and is jauntily rigged out with a Jubilee clock.

When we penetrate into Elie the presence of the invader and the ravages of prosperity proclaim themselves yet more plainly. On the terraces of the new hotel impending over the roadway, guests in knickers and blazers are smoking and talking golf. A family party accost us and, in a tongue on which Glasgow is writ large, inquire the way to the railway station. A bevy of damsels, in killing costumes, issue forth to post letters on the way to the steamboat pier on the Apple Rock. Following in the wake of these, we find the Toll Green become a trim and pretty *alameda*, planted with trees; at the Toft not even a fish-creel lingers to lend the spot a savour of old times; the approaches to the East Links are pervaded by the perambulating nursery-maid. Hunting after the spirit of an Elie that has gone, we enter the churchyard. Here, too, things have been swept and garnished. There is no longer any of the admired disorder of head and table stones with half-obliterated epitaphs, half-buried in the long grass. Still there are slabs with lettering and emblems two centuries old, and the fabric of the Parish Church itself, with its later but quainter spire, built by a Sir John Anstruther at his own expense, reminds us that the burgh is not of yesterday.

What would 'auld Maggie Wud o' the Ailie'—she who 'likit a' things weel but good things best'—have said to it all? Probably, as the local exponent of the philosophy of being pleased with things as you find them, she would have rejoiced in the transformation. This at least is the way with the feck of Elie folk. Still, for a good part of the year—and the observant reader will have noted that by this time we have travelled far into the warm heart of summer as well as into the East of Fife—they can hardly call their town their own; their streets and playgrounds are in the hands of the stranger, and they remain for the most part indoors serving customers.

Elie Parish Church.

A rambler by the fringes of Fife forty years ago had a different story to tell. Elie then wore a melancholy air; it was 'a disappointed place.' It was necessary to assure the visitor,

who might be deceived by first impressions
and the ill word given to it by the Gazetteers,
that it was no more deadly dull than its neighbours.   A generation later came another guest
to Elie—I speak of my old friend and colleague, Dr Charles Cooper, of the *Scotsman*;
and he was delighted with the quiet charm of
this nook of the Kingdom—with its invigorating breezes, its generous endowment of turf
and sand and rock, its glorious outlook upon
the Firth and the Lothian shores, the air of
ease and peace and frank enjoyment pervading
a place where you could 'wear in the afternoon
and evening the same loose coat you had put
on in the morning, and where your wife had
not to dress for parade.'   He put pen to
paper and let his heart overflow in praise of
the most unpretentious and delightful of watering-places.   And then the world—at least the
little world within easy reach of Elie—rushed
in to see and to share in the discovery.   Possibly, were he to come and look upon his
handiwork, he might feel a little sorry that he
had let himself be tempted to blab of his
'Find in Fife.'

> This is no my ain Elie,
> Fair though the Elie be.

The difference is that between a beauty still
unconscious of her power and one that begins
to know her own charms, and is willing to set
them off to the best advantage.

Later we sit down by the rocks fringing the Ruby Bay to smoke the calumet of peace. The colours of day slowly fade from the sky, and out of the sea the mystic grey haze steals in and wraps the land in its folds. The lights of Elie become faint blurs of red and the flashing eye of the May is quenched. It is a medium in which sounds and forms seem to be magnified. Yet nothing is to be seen but the vague shapes of the rocks, and nothing heard except the sob of the troubled breast of the sea as it tells its secret to the shore. An infinite calm falls upon the spirit. Elie satisfies us through and through. We have time to analyse the twinge of mis-content which came upon us when we paced its clean and handsome streets a few hours ago. Partly it was that feeling of disappointment which seizes us when we meet with something else than we had counted on, though it may happen to be something better. As the author of the *Roundabout Papers* has noted, one murmurs even at roast turkey with truffles and champagne if he has set his heart upon an honest beefsteak and a homely pint of stout. Partly, no doubt, the passing pique at Elie was a reflection of the misery which one unfortunate member of the company suffered in having to tramp, through a town where people have become rather point-device in their apparel, in raiment plastered with the mud of the Cocklemill Burn.

ELIE TO CRAIL.

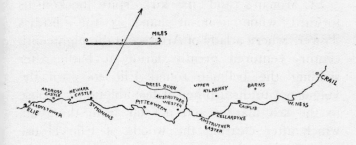

Eastward they scoured, out-scampering the gale,
Till they took refuge in the town of Crail.

TENNANT'S Anster Fair

THE sun is gilding Elie Kirk steeple when
we look abroad the next morning. The
air that is stirring the trees is Elie air—bland yet
stimulating. The mist has drawn off and has
pitched a camp on Kellie Law, whence by and
by it will make a descent and lay waste the
smiling landscape around Balcaskie and Balcarres,
turning green fields and woods and blue sky
and waters into one monotone of grey. In such
weather, bracing and joyous, and yet subject to
sharp and harsh changes of mood, should one

set forth to explore Farthest Fife—that East
Neuk which is the abstract and brief epitome
of the Kingdom, as Fife itself is the concentrated
essence of Scottish history and character.

St Monan's and its kirk spire beckon us
forward, while near at hand is the 'Lady's
Tower,' where a lady of Ardross of the eighteenth
century ventured, greatly daring, to bathe, after
sending the bellman round Elie to warn the
vulgar not to disturb her at her ablutions. Close
to the sea margin and not far from the road,
which after clearing the woods of Elie House
pursues the even tenor of its way between the
open fields, are a fragment or two of the walls
of Ardross Castle, and beside it, and much more
conspicuous, is its doocot. All over Fife the
Columbarium attends the Castle as closely as did
Ralpho Hudibras. With 'the wee pickle land,
the big pickle debt, and the lawsuit,' it made
one of the prime elements of a Fife lairdship.
The Dishingtons of Ardross, however, were not
of the small fry of Fife landowners. The
builder of the castle married a sister of the
Bruce ; and he gave entertainment here to King
David II. and his Queen when they landed from
the wreck on the Lady's Rock, and helped them
to set about fulfilling their vow to erect a church
to their preserver, Monan the Martyr.

A quarter of a mile farther along the shore,
also on the cliff edge, is the gaunt shell of
Newark Castle.   Here lived, when done with

Kirk and State affairs and war's alarms, David Leslie—the victor of Philiphaugh, the vanquished of Dunbar—one of the most distinguished of the long list of soldiers of fortune whom Fife sent out from its narrow bounds to carve their names on continental and national history.

High up is the window of the room where a daughter of the house secretly sheltered and fed a young Lindsay of Balcarres, a hunted rebel of the '15, and, like Grizel Hume of Polwarth, drew upon herself thereby reproaches for her gluttony. The vaults have in their time been well stored with smuggled goods, and brushes with that common enemy of Whig and Jacobite—the gauger—have been witnessed on the shore below.

Beetling over the cliff of greenstone and trap is the inevitable doocot, festooned with salmon nets. You cannot go far along these shores of Fife without seeing the line of stakes running out to sea, the salmon coble in the cove, and the bleached nets drying in the sun.

The footpath between the grain crops and the braeface lands us under the lee of St Monan's Church. There it squats on the west bank of the 'Inweary Burn,' lifting its stumpy grey spire of hewn stone high enough to survey the country round, and turning one of its weather-beaten gables to the sea that in times of storm drenches the great solid retaining wall of its kirkyard. The preservation of his ancient Church, now more than five centuries old, is not the least of the miracles wrought by Monan of the May. He was slain by Northmen, on the island which St Adrian and he and other holy men have made sacred ground, and buried at his chapel 'nere to the se.' An anchorite kept his memory alive in a cell of the rock on the other side of the burn from the site of St Monan's Kirk; and wonderful cures followed the touch of his relics. David Bruce owed more to him than preservation from the angry Firth; for the virtue of Monan's bones had already healed the grievous arrow wound he had got at Neville's Cross.

St Monan's has suffered ill-treatment and neglect. Its north and south transepts stood long roofless; and a Lord Kellie was able to pronounce it 'as decayed and dirty as a Kirk ought to be.' But thanks to the strength of its walls, it was never 'dung doun,' or even abandoned as a place of worship; and when the ancient Kirk of Abercrombie had to be deserted, it was a happy thought, although prompted by thrift, to flit the parish church to this chapel by the sea. Again, in the early part of the century, it was on the point of being condemned and demolished; but its guardian saint, or the rising sense of taste in church architecture, interposed, and it was restored instead to its present form.

In its original shape, this little gem of the middle-pointed Gothic art of its era is said to

Newark Castle.

have been cruciform, with the square tower surmounted by the octagonal spire at the inter-
section of the limbs. But architects tell us
they can find no traces of a nave extending to
the west of the steeple. Such as it is, Fife

St Monan's.

and St Monan's have reason to be proud and
careful of it.

We scramble by the boulders across the bed
of the burn to the fishing village, and run the
gauntlet of its smells towards the harbour.
Concerning the cave of Monan, it contents us
to take the word of a former minister of the
parish, that it is 'a snug recess sheltered by
the tiles and grey eaves of a byre, among
the banks, walls, and ruinous tenements of the
village, overhung by a dusky coloured mass of
high whinstone rock.' It is dead low tide at
the pier—on water and on land. The two or
three boats left in the harbour are aground,
and on shore is only the irreducible minimum

of superannuated loafers and tow-headed and bare-legged bairns.

Life in a fisher-town has its regular ebb and flow like the sea ; and the business of 'St Minnin's' has been on the great waters from time immemorial. Sir Robert Sibbald was able to count, two centuries ago, twelve boats, with seven men each, plying from the port in the herring season. How gladly would one dispense with his dissertation on the identity of the Picts of Fife with the Goths, for the sake of the sketchiest of pictures of the fisher-folk and fisher-life, the boats and tackle and street and quay scenes of the place that lay within an hour's walk of his uncle's house at Gibliston ! Then, as now, the movement of the silvery shoals coming in from the great deep must have sent a thrill and quiver to the adjoining land. In St Monan's the very Kirk bell was tongue-tied when the 'Draive' was off the coast, lest its chime should scare away the fish. They no longer come so near in their myriads. But as faithfully as the tides answer the moon do stir and bustle in and about the harbour respond to the approach of the harvest of the sea. It is a poetess from the southern border of Fife who sings :

> O joyfu's the din when the boats come in,
>   When the boats come in sae early ;
> When the lift is blue, and the herring nets fu',
>   And the sun glints on a' things rarely ;

When the wives buskit braw, and the bairns an' a',
　　Come linkin' doun to the quay, O,
And the very fisher dugs pu' each other by the lugs,
　　And join in the general glee, O.

Then as the fish move farther away, boats and men move after them. The crews are scattered from Cape Clear to the Shetlands, and the villages by the Forth lapse back into torpor. There are times, too, when the mood of the sea rules yet more powerfully the pulse of St Monan's—when hearts beat as wildly as the waves outside with fear and hope and grief, and then sink again into the stony calm of despair.

Strangers with pencil or brush in hand are not ferlies in 'St Minnin's,' and the inhabitants have acquired ideas of their own about art and artists. This we gather from the company of youngsters of both sexes who draw near and audibly and frankly comment upon our appearance and work, as we sit resting and sketching at the corner of the harbour. The local authority already cited was not mistaken when he deplored the prospect of the dulling, through contact with outside influences, of 'the fine edge of delicacy,' still discernible in the fisher-folk of fifty years before. Fortunately a group of the elders of the village, seated within short hail, do not think us worthy of attention, and there is wafted to us, between whiffs of tobacco smoke, snatches of native conversation.

They are posting up somebody who through absence has temporarily lost touch of the village news.

'Did the trip gae to May this year?'

'Humph! Aye; an' got drooned. It was fair weeshin' oot.'

'What's come o' Sandie Reekie?'

'Humph! he's soomin' a steamer on the Tay.'

As we pursue the path by the shore towards Pittenweem we come upon a pretty sea idyll. A four-year-old urchin, naked as when he was born, is seated in a Brobdingnagian toy boat, which he fills from stem to stern, and his older companions tow him backwards and forwards between an outlying ledge and the rocky beach. The radiant young rogue, plump-limbed as a Cupid and fearless as a Mer-baby, grins at us in passing from his rocking craft, which has barely an inch or two of freeboard, and the picture is still in our thoughts when our nostrils are saluted by the scent of the stacks of dried white fish with which Pittenweem has barricaded this western approach to its sea-town.

Verily a gnarled and wind-rooted product of its soil and air is this ancient royal burgh, as viewed from the Shore. The tall and grim old houses fronting the harbour scowl upon the sea as though they had faced nothing but foul weather from that quarter since they were

built. Two, that mount guard at the east end
of the empty quay, are more quaint-looking
than their fellows, and totter a little as if age
and rheumatism had got into their joints. The
rest, drawn up stiffly in line, look like the first
rank of one of those regiments of dour Whiga-
more mariners, salters, and maltsters, who
went forth from the East Neuk to withstand
Montrose and his caterans.

Pittenweem has been a centre of religious
life and a place of trade, but never the abode
of peace. The seed of it, as of St Monan's and
other Fife towns, may be sought in the cave
on the slope of the hill between the priory
ruins and the shore. Doubtless it sheltered
some holy man of the Age of Saints—perhaps
Fillan, of the illuminated armbone; and Pittenweem is 'the settlement of the Cave.' The
grotto has two chambers and a well; and
there are subterranean stairs and passages, now
blocked, that led to the monastic buildings
above. A convent of Austin canons-regular,
dedicated to the Virgin, was planted here in
the twelfth century. It was joined to St
Adrian's fane on the May, and when the
ardour of mediæval monasticism for seclusion
cooled down the monks of the island flitted to
Pittenweem to be nearer their lands and the
world. So the burgh grew around the Priory,
and Town Hall and Parish Church have arisen
within the precincts of the religious house.

Monks and burgesses alike, they had a fine
hearty stomach for a quarrel in Pittenweem.
The Prior and Convent have been seen 'in
arrayit batill,' shooting 'divers pieces of artil-
lerie' at the King's officers, who would have
cut their corn while a lawsuit was pending.
The townsfolk set the fashion of fitting out
privateers to punish the 'English loons' of
pirates. They carried on a long internecine
war, over tolls and dues on fish and malt and
coal, with their neighbour burghs to the east
—the Ansters, Kilrenny, and Crail.

Perhaps it was their too great familiarity with
monkish ways that led the Pittenweem people
to throw themselves with so much zeal into the
cause of the Reformation and later into 'the
business of the Kirk.' Years after Fife's great
Battle of Armageddon, vessels of the burgh were
'lying wrakit in the full sea, the master and haill
mariners being killit at Kilsyth.' Great, too, was
the steer, stramash, and strife in this quarrel-
some nook of the Kingdom when Charles II.—a
crowned and covenanted prince—entered Pittenweem, and the town, remembering its debt to
his grandfather, the kindly pedant who had interested himself in its plague of witches and
gifted to it 'the great house or lodging of the
Monastery,' hoisted its colours on the bartizan of
the tower of the Parish Church, met him with
eight-and-forty of its ablest men in their best
apparel, with partisans and musquets, spread at

The Priory, Pittenweem.

'Robert Smith's yett' a table furnished with, among other cates, 'sundrie great bunns of fine flour,' and broached barrels of its strong home-brewed ale to speed him on his way to Worcester Fight.

In a house in St Mary Street the Kirkcaldy gauger was soundly sleeping, with the proceeds of a sale of smuggled goods captured at Anstruther in his saddle-bags, when Andrew Wilson, the Pathhead baker, and his accomplices broke in upon his rest, and set afoot the fatal business of the 'Porteous Riots.' And, to interpose a somewhat milder memory in Pittenweem's stormy record, Douglas, Bishop of Salisbury, the friend of Johnson and Goldsmith, 'the scourge of imposters, the terror of quacks,' was born in the Water Wynd.

Pittenweem Parish Church.

The relics of the Priory are scattered dispersedly, in the shape of fragments of ivied wall and carven stones built into later dwellings. The residence of the incumbent of the Episcopal Chapel is reared on the site, and partly with the materials of the Monastery. It was the dower-house of the Earls of Kellie, until it came into the possession of that last and admirable example of the nonjuring bishop and table wag of his century, Dr Low. With him may be said to have expired the purest type of East of Fife Jacobitism, although in its more combative form it must have been dying when, in the '45, Lord Kellie was only able to enlist for the regiment that was to have done battle for the rightful Prince one lieutenant-general and one serving-man.

The fighting spirit of Pittenweem may be quenched and its romance faded, but it is a pleasant spot enow, approached from the land side. From it to Anstruther is but a spang, either by the road or by the shore. We make our spang, as usual, by the coast—past the Prior's Saddle, and the bathers splashing where the monks stepped ashore; past Billow Ness, where Pittenweem and Anstruther meet to play golf—on a hazardous little links, made up of turfy tables and rocky gullies—on the spot, dedicated of old to the burning of witches, to which young Chalmers was wont to come and 'preach to the waves.' And we land, as did Rob the Ranter and so many other pilgrims bound to the 'Lint Fair' in the Loan, in the green behind the shore houses of Wester Anster, and, by and by, at the trees and bridge shadowing the drumly waters of the Dreel Burn.

Were it not for the Dreel one could not tell where Wester Anstruther ends and Easter

Anstruther begins; and between the latter and Cellardyke, the shore part of the burgh of Kilrenny, there is only the narrower ribbon of the 'Culdies Burn.' These little East of Fife towns, from Earlsferry to Crail, are strung together like 'herrings on a hake'; or should we say, looking to their past and their present, like a row of extinct volcanoes?

The Ansters and Lower Kilrenny are volcanoes run together, like craters in the moon. They monopolise the shore for a mile and a half, and make no secret that their business is in fish. Their debt to the sea is proclaimed on the arms of these venerable burghs, who were driving a lucrative trade with the Low Countries, curing herrings and salting cod when Liverpool was a place of small account, and the town-herd of Glasgow drove the cattle of the burgesses afield to the site of the new City Hall. Pittenweem bears a figure of Adrian in his boat; Kilrenny a fisher-craft rowing under sun and cloud; Crail a masted galley with stars; Easter Anster an anchor.

The Wester burgh rejoices in the device of three salmon. As we enter by the West Port we note, as a freak of local taste, that spoils of the sea are plastered on the very house-fronts, in the shape of *buckies* and cockles arranged in geometric patterns. We note also that wealth and variety of occupation must have increased since 1617, when the magistrates sought to excuse themselves from regaling the sovereign with beef, on the plea that it was 'ane very mean town, yea, of all the burghs of this realm the meanest,' wherein 'not ane flesher' was to be found, 'we being all seafaring men and fishers.' The dumpy Parish Church still stands in its churchyard by the Dreel, but the 'Craw's Nest' of Fisher Willie and later lairds of Anstruther, in which Charles II. supped to his liking, has long disappeared from the other bank. The Church itself, probably pre-Reformation in date, has suffered restoration that has cleared out the old trade lofts, and all that was quaint and characteristic of the former life of the burgh—worse havoc this than when the 'Inglis' landed at Anster, plundered the Kirk of its sand-glass, and flung 'ye auld bybell in ye sea.'

Easter Anster Kirk is almost within hail. Younger than its neighbour—younger by a full generation even than the manse which worthy Maister James Melvill, nephew of Andrew, the Boanerges of St Rule's, perfected with his own hands in 1590—it has suffered less from the improver, and its curious lopsided tower, crowned by a weather-beaten bartizan and abbreviated spire, is pleasant to look upon. Two years before he completed his manse Maister James chronicles, in his inimitable way, an incident that startled Anstruther. For a remnant of the ruined Armada—no other than Juan Gomez de Medina, general of twenty hulks, and his ship-

wrecked crews—were drifted hither from Fair
Isle, and landed 'nocht to giff mercy bot to ask.'
The minister was brought from his bed to talk
with them, and held courteous discourse with a
Spaniard of 'grave and stout
countenance,' who ' bekkit
even to the yeard'; and
behind were, ' to the number
of thirteen score, for the
maist part young beardless
men, silly, trauchled, and
hungered,' whom Anstruther
feasted on 'kail, porridge,
and fish '—an unwonted but
welcome diet for the castaway dons; even when
seasoned by godly Maister
James's discourse on 'the
words of the Prophet Elisa
to the King of Israel in
Samaria—Give them bread
and water.'

Easter Anster Kirk.

Most of the streets of
Anster find their way down
to the Fore Shore. It is
spacious, like the harbour which it borders, and
the fine row of tall houses behind the Town
Cross has a certain Batavian grace, reflected,
one fancies, from some Flemish quay or market-
place where Anster did business before the Union
spoiled its shipping trade,

On the road down to it you pass close to the house where Thomas Chalmers was born, one of the fourteen children of a substantial dyer and shipowner of the place. John Goodsir, the anatomist, and William Tennant, who has sung with such birr and gusto and nimble fancy the humours of 'Anster Fair,' were likewise natives; not to mention the more—nay most—doubtful case, cited by a friend, of Chaucer's poor scholars of 'Soler halle of Cantebregge,' Johan and Alayn,

> Of a town were they born that hyght Struthir,
> Fer in the North, I can nat telle where.

Of Tennant we got a glimpse through the eyes of one who had seen him—'a mere apology for a man, but a gentleman every inch.' Anster folk still point out the spot in the East Green where stood Maggie Lauder's change-house; but do not seem to remember so well the site of William Cockburn's low-ceilinged stationer's shop on the Shore, where, when the Great French War was raging and the newfangled stage-coach was a marvel of swiftness, the news of the day was dispensed to the half-pay naval captains and Tory lairds who made it their howff, while young Archibald Constable served them from behind the counter with sealing-wax, blotting sand, and goose quills.

Through the long mean street of Cellardyke goes our road, skirting Skinfast-haven. Where that dingy fisher-town tapers to nothing, and inside the gleaming teeth of the Wolves and Cutty Skelly rocks, are the 'Cardinal's Steps.' David Beaton was wont to disembark at them on his way to St Andrews or to visit his lands around Cellardyke. Kilrenny, the Upper, whose spire peeps at us over the slope, has, or thinks it has, in its churchyard the grave of the 'proud Cardinal' whom Norman Leslie and his company first murdered and then pickled in salt. It is a tiny hamlet that became a royal burgh by a blunder, and then annexed Cellardyke to ballast itself with population.

Paul Jones once anchored off Cellardyke, and, disappointed in his hope of finding a pilot among the fishermen, fired a round shot ashore, which long after was picked out of the sod of what is now the school playground.

There are still three miles of a delightful walk, by a shore haunted by sea-birds and strewn with boulders, to the 'ancient well-aired toun o' Crail.' Half-way are the Coves and Hermit Well of Caiplie.

A projecting rock, with the profile of a lion's face, is hollowed into dark cells, on the walls of which incised crosses and other symbols are traced. This is 'Caplauchy,' where Peden, the Covenanter, hid his head—where Adrian and his companions, coming from the Land of Hungarie, 'arrivit intil Fife,' before passing to the May Island, that lies abreast of the Cave, and kindling there a flame that shone over Pictish Scotland.

Should we not couple with this light-bringing mission the work of the Laird of Barns—the father of the bride of Drummond of Hawthornden, that died while her wedding feast was being got ready—who first raised on the May a beacon to guide the mariner entering the Firth? The island priory, to which sick pilgrims and barren women once flocked, is but a fragment of old wall; Cunningham's 'coal lowe' is replaced by an electric light, that flashes its message across sixty miles of sea. But the memory of good deeds remains.

As we peer into the Caiplie Cave a young damosel of Crail, and the visitor she has brought in tow, peer beside us.

'A poor specimen,' he says disparagingly of the local lion.

'A poor one, but our own. Big enough for Crail,' is the tart retort.

Nymphs of remotest Fife—

> Seu vos Pittenweema tenent, seu Crelia crofta,
> Sive Anstræa domus—

your voices, heard in the dusk, sound sweetly, yet with capabilities of sharpness, as when Drummond walked with his Mary by the Coves of Caiplie and the Castlehaven Braes and dressed up into his Latin macaronics the flytings of two neighbouring lairds' wives!

Pittenweem.

II

CRAIL TO ST ANDREWS.

Hitherto shalt thou come, but no further.

Book of Job.

THE windows of the East Neuk Hotel look out upon the Westgait of Crail. Opposite, the Crosscauseway leaves the clean, wide thoroughfare, and winds down, among gable-ends and forestairs, towards the harbour, and sends off a branch that climbs round the Castle walls to the terrace overlooking the sea. Above the roofs and chimneys there is a glint of blue waters. If you step down into the roadway, the chances are that you will have it all to yourself. Farther eastward there is a twist in the street, where it dodges round a quaintly corbelled corner and the vista is nearly closed by the Town House Steeple; and then it becomes broader still as, under the name of the High Street and the Marketgait, it passes the Market Cross and the Kirk. Parallel, and nearer the sea, is another spacious thoroughfare —the Nethergait—with a passage or two diving down from it to the shore.

Half an hour's walk, from where Crail opens liberal portals to let the east wind enter and wrestle with the trees it has planted in its chief streets, brings you to Fifeness—the Ultima Thule of the Kingdom—beyond which there is no land until you come to Denmark. There is no hurry yet to take that road. Let us stroll leisurely round this ' Fortress in the Nook.'

And first down towards the harbour. It is set in a wrinkle of the rocky coast, and the steep braes and the clusters of houses that scramble up their face impend over the narrow quay. Roome Bay, a furlong or two eastward, would have afforded more spacious harbourage. But this is ' big enough for Crail.' The schooner and the fishing-craft or two in the tiny haven are 'oxtered' close into the land. The sea wall is thrust out and wound round them like a strong arm shielding them from the blasts of the North Sea. Two ghostly sentinels mount guard at different levels on the cliff behind; they are whitewashed obelisks, bearing the guiding lights of the harbour. From the angle of the high walls enclosing the site of the Royal Castle projects a look-out turret that almost overhangs the pier. Behind it is a patch of greenery, shorn close down to the level of the protecting walls by the keen scythe

Crail Harbour.

of the east wind; and immediately below is the terrace where Crail can take the air and watch what is passing in the haven beneath.

It has been a seaport and fishing-place for a thousand years. The time when it first learned the art of curing herrings and traded in them to the Netherlands is lost in the mists of antiquity. King Constantine may have been gnawing a 'Crail capon' when he spied from this watch-tower of the Kingdom the coming of the terrible Northmen; and doubtless it was a toothsome dish at the board of David the Saint, William the Lion, Malcolm the

Maiden, and Robert the Bruce, all of whom are said to have visited and favoured Crail.

Long after it ceased to be a kingly hunting-seat and residence the shadow of royalty clung to Crail. Its Hereditary Constables had authority from the Water of Leven to the 'Brook Puttiken.' It supplied the royal table with 'rabbits, herring, and porpoises.' There is nothing left of the fabric of the Castle or of the Chapel of St Rufus, once enclosed within its precincts; and only a fragment down beside the shore of the Nunnery of Crail, which had Haddington as its mother-house.

But so long as Crail has its Collegiate Church with its churchyard it will be unable to forget that it has a past behind it. The tumble-down school-house has lately been removed that screened the Kirk from the Market-gait, and you now look freely into an enclosure which is more richly endowed with memorials of former generations, in crumbling mural tombs and mossgrown head and through stones, than perhaps any other country God's Acre in Scotland. At the corner of the high-way is the 'Blue Stone of Crail.' It is the local fetish; and Crail bairns used to kiss it in leaving the old town, in pledge of their return. Satan—who, first and last, has had much to do with the raising of Fife kirks— flung it at the steeple from the Isle of May, where he sat girning and gnashing his teeth after being caught in the act of laying hands to the sacred building; in witness whereof his thumb-mark is to be seen to this day on the big boulder.

When this incident happened cannot be told exactly. But in 1517 William Myrton, Vicar of Lathrisk, aided by the Abbess of Hadding-ton, endowed the Church as a collegiate charge, with a provost and nine prebends, who served in the different chapels under its broad roof dedicated to the Virgin and saints. Over one of its altars was the wonder-working 'Auld Rude of Karrail'; the town became far known for miracles and pilgrimages as well as for 'speldrins and partans.'

Changes and flittings came in the train of John Knox, who began here in June 1559 his crusade against the monuments of Papacy. A few months later we find the 'juggis counsaill and haill communitie amyaberly desyring the haill chaplains of the town to apply thame selfis to Goddis word, and lyf godily, conform to the Congregation.' There were Crail folk who did not take 'amyaberly' to the new dis-pensation. John Melvill—brother of Andrew of St Andrews, and uncle of James of Anster —was preaching in the Kirk a savoury dis-course touching 'that filthy swine the Bishop of Rome,' when a Bailie's wife 'rase in the essemble and with hech voce said aganis hym thyr wordis: "It is a schame to yow that ar gentillmen that ye pull hym nocht owt of the pulpot be the luggis."'

Crail Church.

Let us be thankful that the fabric survived these and later ecclesiastical storms—that the venerable steeple lifts its severe lines, a land-mark over leagues of sea; that the bell in the tower, cast by Peeter Vanden Ghein in

1614, still calls the worshippers to prayer; that the Sculptured Stone, oldest of Crail's relics, no longer prone on the pavement, presents to them as they enter a face traced with strange symbols of bird and beast and creeping thing, and that within there are still a fragment or two of carved oak panelling and other mementoes of the generations who have come and gone.

But it is on the churchyard walls that Crail's history is writ large and full. He who prowls round them, especially if he has been looking into Mr Erskine Beveridge's admirable work, can read in the quaint lettering of this Book of the Dead the story of the rise and fall in the fortunes of the burgh and of its leading families. The oldest and finest of its group of mural tombs is a monument also of the Dutch intercourse with Crail in the end of the sixteenth century. It is to a hot-blooded Lumsden of Airdrie, who got into trouble by meddling with the Crown jewels and with the plots of Francis, Earl of Bothwell, and it was raised in the year when the East Neuk lairds were setting afoot their perilous enterprise of colonising the Lews, that brought them more bastonings than profit. The reigns of the Sixth James and the First Charles must have been a prosperous time for the burgesses of Crail—for merchants in fish and malt, like the Bailie, 'of doughty Douglas Kyn,' whose tomb

declares that he 'lived in all men's love,'
although extant records attest that on occasion
he took the law into his own hands. Fair
monuments of the period have sprouted thickly
along the west and south walls—among them
the broken effigy of a knight, in plate armour,
long identified by Crail as its benefactor The
Bruce, but found by sober research to be only
a Bruce of Symbister, who went to the
Orkneys and pushed his fortunes under the
savage Earls Robert and Patrick, and came
back to die in this pleasant nook.

With the Civil War and the troubles of
the Covenant discord and poverty fell on the
burgh, and the monuments wax few and mean.
But here is a memorial to 'Lang Sandy
Leslie,' with whom Archbishop Sharp smoked
his last pipe at Ceres, before crossing Magus
Moor, and who came, like Sharp before him,
to be minister of Crail, until, at the Revolution,
he was turned out for refusing to pray for
their Majesties William and Mary. Rank
Jacobitism lingered long beside bitter Whiggery
in these parts; and Lord Rosebery's 'judicious
Crawford, who got a pension from George
and a knighthood from James,' was a portioner
and bailie in Crail. To a later, and from the
point of view of sepulchral art, a debased era,
belong Jamie Kingo's rhyming lingos and the
praises of the Classic M'Min.

At the door of the Town Hall we pause,

looking up at a fragment of an older Tolbooth
bearing the burgh arms—a ship of exaggerated
Dutch build, terribly overmanned and over-
burdened by her crew of full-faced mariners—

Crail Town Hall.

while the Provost (douce man!) fumbles at the
door and mystifies us with the promise of a
sight of the 'bulls wi' dauds o' wax hingin'
at the tails o' them,' kept there under lock

and key. They are Papal Bulls of Julian II. and Leo X., in the beautiful bold caligraphy of their age and country; and here also we have a peep at the ancient bell 'lifted' from the Kirk and hung in the queer pagoda-like tower; at the battered old iron-clasped chest that formerly held the burgh archives; and at other curious municipal antiquities.

The Chief Magistrate himself may well rank as one of these, for he tells us that he is the senior by six months of Mr Gladstone, and is still in the thick of politics. Many kindnesses and much local lore are showered on us by Crail's Grand Old Man and by other citizens, and we depart after having kissed, in spirit, the Blue Stone and vowed to return to this trimmest and most venerable and also last of the little burghs sewed round the southern hem of Fife.

For, out and alas! our peregrination of this part of Fife draws, for the time, to a close. At St Andrews must we call a halt. Our tracing of the fringes began on the banks of a drumly tidal river, rolling slowly between its carselands; it is arrested where the waves of the North Sea beat restlessly on an iron coast. It began when frost bound the earth, and set a keen edge to the wind; it ends with a July sun blazing down out of a blue sky.

A last and choice morsel is left. Fifeness has still to be weathered; the shoreward edges of the links of Balcomie, the woods of Cambo, and the braes of Kinkell to be traced. The path to the East Neuk winds round the curve of Roome sands and traverses Crail's golf-course, 'usit for pastime and sundrie kinds of exercise' by the burghers of three centuries ago. The gravestones of an ancient cell of St Monan bridge the burn and prop the grain stacks of Kilminning. Mount the bank, and across the fields you will see the dark tower of Balcomie, weirdest of aspect and most remote of situation of all the Castles of the Thanedom, built by a Learmonth of the 'Rhymer's kin.' From it rode once another Laird of Balcomie —a Sir William Hope, author of *The Complete Fencing Master*—to meet and slay, by the Sculptured Stone of Sauchope hard by, a stranger-guest who had come from foreign parts to test his unrivalled skill as a horseman and swordsman. Farther off is Wormiston. The family of Spens, who wonned there for centuries, claimed descent from the Thanes of Fife, and were Hereditary Constables of Crail. Sir Patrick, of the grand old ballad, may have been a branch of this wind-rooted tree. It fell, or was transplanted to Scandinavia, and then the Lindsays—'more Royalist than the King —came to Wormiston, and have left their arms and initials sprinkled plentifully over the door-way and windows of their old mansion hidden among the trees.

And now we reach the last land-hold of Old Romance—the very sanctuary of the East Wind. The great rocks, as we move forward to the Cape Turnagain of Fife, look as if they had been cracked and split by the hammer of Thor before the sea began to wear them smooth. Every jutting point has its cap of white, and from every hollow comes a murmur of waves. The breeze prowls, keen and unsatisfied, even at this warm summer noontide, over the braes and round the boulders, and—

> Out and in, out and in,
> Bends the bush and whirls the whin.

The stones of the ‘Dane’s Dyke’ are grey with lichen and patched with moss. The hands of the sea-rovers who built it a thousand years ago are mouldering under the close wiry grass and patches of bent, heather, and sea pinks. Thinner grows the covering, and more and more the naked ribs of the rock protrude, until, like a great ploughshare, the Ness plunges down into the sea and marks with a white furrow the track towards the Carr Lightship and ‘Norrowa’ over the Faem.’

A group of sun-browned lasses in clean pinafores are round the draw-well; little reck they, or we as we drink from their hands, that its waters have mingled with the blood of Dane and Scot. The picnickers have been before us at the Black Cave—the Nigra Specus of the old Chroniclers—and the soot of their fires is over the crosses graven above the stone pillow on which Constantine lay dying, having fought and lost his last battle with the heathen by the Northern Sea. On the Blue Rock—a fragment of the pebble the Foul Fiend flung at Crail Kirk—we stripped to bathe in the sandy bay, where Mary of Guise landed with her French courtiers, to become the wife of James V. and the mother of Mary Stuart.

Then, with faces turned towards St Andrews, we pursue the rough and scrambling shore path, past the gaunt shape of Randerston Castle, the former home of the Myrtons, which lifts a turretted shoulder above the level of the braes ; by the parks and rabbit-warrens of Cambo, where a pleasant diversion is made inland, to bait at the cosy village of Kingsbarns on cheese and bread ; and across the Pitmilly Burn—the 'Brook Puttiken' of the Crail charters.

> Blaw the weather as it likes,
> There's beild aboot Pitmilly dykes.

Having outflanked the Kenley Burn, on whose banks no stone could we find upon another of the palace of Inchmurtach, where the Bishops of St Andrews were wont to feast the Kings who came here to hunt the boar, we ask only beild from the blazing sun as we pause to wipe perspiring foreheads at Buddo Ness. We look across St Andrews Bay, where a fishing smack is tacking close inshore, to the vision of the tall towers and crooked pinnacles of the city of St Regulus, written against the horizon—

Like a Turk verse upon a scimitar.

St Andrews from Buddo Ness.

It is the goal of this stage of our Fife pilgrimage; and at the sight of it memories come crowding of the saints and martyrs, the kings and prelates, the plotters and zealots, the men great in war, in letters, and in golf who have played their parts on that narrow platform by the sea. But before we present ourselves at the old Abbey gateway, 'Craigduff' and the 'Rock and Spindle' have been climbed, and a wide berth has been given to the 'Maiden.' 'Be bold, but not too bold,' we seem to read on the time-worn portal of Prior Hepburn's Walls; and we enter.

ST ANDREWS.

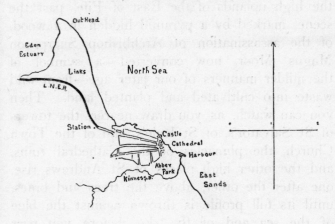

Saint Andrews by the Northern Sea,
A haunted town thou art to me.

ANDREW LANG.

MANY are the ways, of the flesh and of
the spirit, by which one can approach
and enter St Andrews. Let us rehearse some
of them, in reflective mood, as we climb the
uphill and winding road, between the Priory
acres and the Cathedral stones, to The Pends,
and, from the centre of this grey old city, set
on a promontory of a promontory, in the nook
of a nook, gaze along the vista of South Street,
its chief thoroughfare, where also lies the heart
of its story.

You may journey to it by the means still

used by the majority of its visitors, in spite of
the intrusion of motor bus, car, and cycle—by
the railway, through Leuchars, or by way of
Crail. Or you can descend on it by road from
the high uplands of the East of Fife, past the
scene, marked by a pyramid hidden in a wood,
of the assassination of Archbishop Sharp, on
Magus Moor, now converted—a symbol of
the milder manners of our later age—from wild
waste into cultivated and planted land. Then
you can watch, as you draw nearer, the towers
of St Salvator's, of St Rule's, and of the Town
Church, the pinnacles of the Cathedral ruins,
and the other high places of St Andrews rise,
one after the other, above the trees and braes,
until its full profile is thrown against the blue
of the sea and of the sky, before you pass
through its extra-mural Garden City, and enter
in by its West Port. Or, being a pilgrim
drawn to the Shrine of Golf, you may choose
to see it first, and oftenest, from the side of
the famous Links, in which case, if you are
a confirmed votary of the cleek and brassie,
the College spire, or the north-west tower of
the Castle, will be no more to you than a mark
giving the right direction to one of the in-coming
holes.

If, however, you be a wanderer on foot, seeking to steer a direct course into the middle and
the marrow of St Andrews history, it is best
to draw near it, as we did, out of the east,

St Andrews Cathedral.

and by way of the Kinkell Braes, the East
Sands, and the creek at the mouth of the
Kinness Burn, where the Lang Pier throws
out an arm to shelter a haven that is now the
resort of only a handful of fishing and pleasure
craft. Something can be said in favour of an
approach by sea, and for making acquaintance
with the scene of so many fateful happenings
in Kirk and State from the side whence,
according to tradition, it was first seen by
Regulus, a monk from Achaia, when he carried
hither the relics of the Apostle Andrew—'three
fingers and two toes'—in the fourth—or was it
the ninth?—century; or by Acca of Hexham,
when, as says a rival legend, he fled to Muck-
ross—the 'Boars Chase'—some time in the
seventh century, bearing with him similar
authentic material on which to build the reputation for sanctity that has since adhered to the
spot. By sea also, a thousand years later, more
or less, came back John Knox to the place
he had left as a galley-slave, to deal the first
smashing blow in the Scottish Reformation.

Then having, by land or water, reached the
portal—the old 'Sea Yett'—in the lofty Abbey
Walls, built around the precincts by Prior John
Hepburn, and completed by his nephew and
successor, the notorious Bishop Patrick Hepburn
of Moray, one might well have paused to con-
sider whether to follow the line of its many
towers, gates, and bastions, still adorned with

the arms and initials of its founders, and to join, at the bridge over the burn, the main stream of modern traffic that flows through Abbey Street into the core of St Andrews. Or, on the principle of beginning at the beginning, should we not rather have turned to the right, behind the old inns and storehouses that mount guard over the deserted harbour, and, averting eyes and noses from the Tophet of the Gasworks, whose smoke and fumes are still permitted to profane the St Andrews 'Holy of Holies,' climb to the little platform overlooking the pier and the sea—which has already gnawed away its predecessor, 'St Mary on the Rock,' and is busy nibbling at its own foundations— where are the lower courses of the buildings and a few grave slabs marking the site of the Celtic Chapel on the Kirkheugh, the earliest of the city's antiquities? For here, or hereabout, if all tales are true, Bishop Cellach preached to king and people long before the relics of Andrew came to land, and when the settlement was known as Kilrymont, the 'Church of the King's Hill.' Here, too, was the latest refuge of the Culdees, whose ecclesiastical authority and possessions, almost whose memory, became merged in the later and greater state of the mediæval Roman Church that enthroned itself behind the monastic wall outside of which stands this forlorn relic of the past.

On the whole, however, we decide that we

have chosen the better part by making straight
for the 'Golden Gate' of St Andrews—the
double archway of the ancient portal of the

The Pends, St Andrews.

House of Augustinian Canons, founded in 1144
by Bishop Robert—and emerging in 'the middle
of things,' beside the shattered west front of

the Cathedral, and in full view of the clean, bright prospective of South Street, lined with dignified three and four-storeyed buildings and by the fresh foliage of young lime-trees. Although stripped of its groined roof and many of its rich mouldings, the 'Pends' gateway remains a noble monument of the taste and skill of the old builders, and is happy prelude to the other architectural glories of the place. It ushers us to what has been for centuries the battlefield of conflicting creeds, languages, customs and ideas—to the spot where took place the tug of war between Monasticism and the New Learning, between the Papacy and the Reformation, between Prelacy and Presbytery, Intrusion and Non-Intrusion.

Past and Present meet and shoulder each other in what time has made not inharmonious conjunction. Within a few yards of us are the Cathedral ruins, 'dung down' successively by tempest, fire, and the hands of man, but still lifting aloft gaunt arms, as if in protest against its fate, and the still grimmer and gloomier fragments of St Leonard's College and Chapel, where George Buchanan taught, Andrew Melville disputed, and John Knox sought brief recreation from strenuous preaching in the Town Kirk, between the three of them kindling and fanning the great purging and destructive fire of the Reformation. A door or two away is the dwelling traditionally identified as that in which dwelt Mary Stuart, in what were perhaps the happiest and most care-free passages of her life as Queen of Scotland. She was but two-and-twenty when she came first to St Andrews and 'lived merrily, like a burgess wife;' and the shadows of care and of doom had scarcely begun to fall on her bright head. The air of this quiet old seat of learning appears to have agreed with her, and she came back to it repeatedly. The house opposite, with the pointed and ogee doorways, and battlemented roundel, projecting into the street, might seem, from its outward looks, to agree better with her story; or the venerable dwelling, with courtyard, draw-well, and heraldic gateway, round the corner in the 'Dean's Court'—the Inn or Manse of the Archdeacon, where once lived George Douglas, who helped Mary to escape from her prison in Lochleven.

The 'Queen's House' turns, however, a much more picturesque side towards its garden, in which Samuel Johnson pretended to discover, in an ancient sycamore, since deceased, the only tree in Scotland older than himself, and towards St Leonard's College to which it is being annexed. From the somewhat lowering shades of the portal of that seat of study, issue a troop of schoolgirls whose bright faces and academic robes—black, trimmed with blue—are in contrast to the dingy grey walls of the Chapel, which bears, like so many other stones of St Andrews, the arms and insignia of its founder, Prior Hepburn, whose grave slab, along with that of the adaptable Superintendent Winram, has been somewhat doubtfully identified among the battered monuments within.

St Leonard's College dates from 1512, and stands on the site of the Guest House of the Priory. In succession a hospice for pilgrims and a nunnery, it was launched on a new career when Hepburn and Archbishop Alexander Stewart, the natural son of James IV., who fell by his father's side on Flodden Field, endowed it as a seminary for poor students. Behind it stood the 'New Inn,' or *Hospitium Novum*, still represented by an archway bearing the Royal Arms of Scotland. It was built hastily for the entertainment and health of Magdalen, the fair but perishing Flower of France, who lived but six weeks after transplantation to the harsher air of Scotland, and whose husband, James V., rapidly consoled, brought hither, within a year, a successor in Mary of Loraine, the mother of the Queen of Scots. The latest seed planted in this secluded space within the Abbey walls has been the St Leonard's School for Girls, and it has thriven mightily.

After combination with St Salvator's, as the United College, the buildings of St Leonard's fell into disuse and decay. It has fared otherwise with its former rival, St Mary's, which, like 'Queen Mary's thorn-tree,' embraced within the reposeful beauty of its Quadrangle, still puts forth green leaves. The façade which it presents to the street has carved upon it, along with the Royal Arms, the shields of the Chancellors of the most ancient of the Scottish universities, from that of its founder, Bishop Wardlaw, down to the latest, Earl Haig. St Mary's, the Divinity School of St Andrews, dates from 1537, but the University, which may be said to function within and around this mellow enclosure, where it had its origin in a 'Pedagogy,' or 'Studium Generale,' and where it continues to hold its ceremonies and to guard, among its other treasures and heirlooms, its maces and its portraits of celebrated Principals, Professors, and students, its Library and its Museum, is older than any of its Colleges, and goes back to 1411.

Alongside the College is the modern Town Hall. Thus do ancient enemies conform to latter-day conditions, and adjust themselves in amicable neighbourhood. The Town Hall once occupied nearly the whole width of the adjoining Market Street, long known as the 'Hie Gait,' overlooking the spot where the annual Lammas Fair, now declined to a shadow of its former self, was held. The Old Tolbooth, beside which was executed a Lord President of the Court of Session, Sir Robert Spottiswoode, son of the Archbishop, for the part he took in Montrose's Rising, obstructed business, and its successor has had to 'toe the line' in the more spacious air of South Street, where, to visitors, it can show, along with the names and portraits of a famous line of Provosts, and other relics of the past, the axe that has done such execution in shearing the heads of the malefactors and others who have presumed to disturb the peace of the burgh and of the realm.

On the other side of the way is an object still more worthy of respectful survey. The Parish or Town Church, dedicated to the Holy Trinity, has a history that is coeval with that of the Cathedral, and was founded by Turgot, the first Catholic Bishop, the confessor and biographer of Saint Margaret, in the beginning of the twelfth century. Of the building that rose three hundred years later, the sturdy steeple is nearly all that makes any outward show. Within, as without, it was thoroughly 're-edified' at the end of the first decade of the present century; and it is now a building of almost Cathedral proportions, richly stored with stained glass and with monuments, among which, overtopping all else in dimensions if not in taste, is the tomb that holds the remains, and proclaims the virtues and the tragic end, of Archbishop Sharp. The ecclesiastics of St Andrews, pre-Reformation and post-Reformation alike—and Sharp not least—have furnished to the world of their own and of later days, singularly abundant materials for praise, pity, and censure. A sermon on the vanity of human ambition, and on the nemesis that waits on evil passions could be preached from the Bishop's Monument, and from the 'Bishop's Branks,' which is also among the antiquities of the Town Church of St Andrews. The ruthless and savage act of the fanatical assassins recoiled not only on their own heads but on the 'Cause of the Covenant;' while the edge of sympathy for the victim and his friends was blunted by the unscrupulous ferocity with which revenge was afterwards pursued in the name of justice.

For the rest, the building is crowded with memories of those who, in good or evil times, have preached and worshipped in it. Knox comes first of all, but there are others of scarcely less account in the annals of the Scottish Church and State, among them Andrew Melville, Alexander Henderson, and Samuel Rutherford, and of a later and happier age, Chalmers, and Tulloch, and A. K. H. Boyd, whose names are written ineffacably in the story of the Town Kirk of St Andrews.

The list of the antiquities of the South Street is far from exhausted. For, moving farther west, we light upon a fine Gothic fragment—apse-like in form, and shaded by a noble group of ashes in the grounds of the Madras College, the bequest of Dr Andrew Bell—that was part of the north transept of the Church of the Dominican or Blackfriars. Of its neighbour,

West Port, St Andrews.

the Greyfriars, almost the only relic that survives is the draw-well of the monastery in a garden adjoining Market Street. But while all the other 'ports' at this western boundary of old St Andrews have been long cleared out of the path of traffic, the West Port stoutly holds its place in the fairway, and those who would enter South Street at this end must, as at The Pends, pass under the vaulting of a mediæval arch, bearing in this case, however, not the marks of the Church artificer, but the impress of the municipal spirit, in the shape of the city arms—the Boar and Oak and St Andrew extended on his Cross, and a group showing David I. riding into the town to confer on it the privileges it continues to cherish.

All the main streets of St Andrews radiate from, or converge towards, the Cathedral. They have been likened to the spokes of a wheel, or the ribs of a fan. Might not the three—or, if we reckon the Scores, once known as the Sparrowgait, the four—wide rays that stretch and spread out of the sacred East be regarded as the fingers of Andrew, held out in apostolic blessing over the city of which, for more than a thousand years, he has been the Patron Saint? All of these avenues were at one time, like South Street, stoppered by a gate, or 'Port,' and as each thoroughfare differed from its neighbour in length, shape, and volume, they might also be compared to the pipes of a great organ, proclaiming, in varied notes, the praise and glory of St Andrews.

Passing over Market Street, which, though central in position and busy of aspect on market days, has been stripped of much of its distinctive features since the removal of its fifteenth-

century Tolbooth—and besides, fails to reach all
the way to the Cathedral—we turn steps and
faces eastward again through North Street.
An air of academic, almost of cloistral seclusion,
invades mind and sense, and is scarcely disturbed by the new and solid blocks of hewn
masonry that are rising on either hand, or by
the vivid patches of colour scattered by the
stream of students of both sexes that is issuing
into the bright sunlight from the dark porch
of the 'College of the Scarlet Gown.' For
these fresh touches on an old-time picture—
the garb of the graduates as well as the
stately mass of the Younger University Hall,
with its adjacent hospices—may be taken
as appurtenances of 'the triumphant College
of St Salvator,' and as sign of the living and
growing vigour of the oldest of Scottish universities.

Sedate and reserved is the aspect of North
Street, but no longer dingy and desolate, as in
the days, about the beginning and middle of
the eighteenth century, when St Andrews was
little more than a deserted village—when, as
Defoe notes, grass was growing between the
stones of its streets, and its university was
lying under threat of extinction, or of removal
to Perth. Crowstepped gables and forestairs
are more in evidence than shopfronts and sign-
boards; and over against the time-grimed
tower and the gothic windows and buttresses of

the Chapel of St Salvator's and the entrance to the quadrangle of the United College, North Street attains to spaciousness. Plenty of room here ' for the crowd who assembled round the portal of the Auld College '—the title it has earned and kept by reason of its seniority, by nearly a century, to St Mary's—to witness, in 1528, the burning of Patrick Hamilton, whose smoke infected a kingdom.

Bishop Kennedy, of whom Dr Hay Fleming, the ' Old Mortality ' of the story of St Andrews, says that ' perhaps he was the only one of its Bishops who has run the risk of incurring the woe pronounced against those of whom all men speak well,' was its founder, and continues to be its presiding genius. His arms are on door and gateway, and his lofty and magnificent tomb of blue sandstone, curiously and intricately wrought by foreign artists, is still the chief glory of the interior, notwithstanding the damage done to it when the vaulted stone roof, needlessly and carelessly removed, collapsed and destroyed many of the monuments underneath. The good Bishop has left in his College other memorials, in the Bell, named ' Kate Kennedy ' —tocsin of student gatherings—and his Mace, later of date, but more elaborate in workmanship than the pair in St Mary's. There may also be seen the carved pulpit of John Knox, shifted hither from the Town Church ; the fifteenth century graveslab of Hugh Spens, who succeeded the historian John Major in the Principalship of the College ; and the silver arrow, for which generations of St Andrew's alumni, including, mayhap, the Great Marquis of Montrose, have contended at the Butts near by.

In front of the Old College Chapel were a good place in which to recite selections from the passages 'in praise of St Andrews,' which the late Professor Knight gathered into a book. So long ago as 1491 foreign visitors are found speaking of its 'famous and imposing' University, its crowds of learned men, its rich and valuable collection of books. To come nearer to our own time, Lord Cockburn considered that Scotland contained no spot equally full of historical interest ; no place 'over which the Genius of Antiquity presides so impressively.' In the eyes of Thomas Carlyle, 'you have there the essence of all the antiquity of Scotland in good clean condition.' Dean Stanley regarded its group of ruined buildings as 'unrivalled in the British Isles, save on the Rock of Cashel, concentrating in one focus, on the extremity of Fife, the successive stages of Northern ecclesiastical polity.'

It has been called the Oxford of the North, and the late Lord Bute makes acknowledgment that it is the only place in Scotland whose appearance can boast any kinship with the University city on the Isis, which 'would

be proud enough of the tower and chapel of
St Salvator, never had any building resembling
the Cathedral, even in its ruins, and has
nothing to compare to the tower of St Regulus
and no walls like those of Prior Hepburn'—
besides all which, Oxford cannot boast of the
'glittering haze of heroic myth' that St
Andrews possesses as background to its recorded annals. According to this authority it
is even more eminent in its names than in its
architecture; and there is scarcely one great
figure in Scottish history that is not associated
with it.

Or hear again another in the long and
brilliant list of its Lord Rectors, Dean Stanley:
'Two voices sound in this secluded sanctuary
of ancient wisdom, with the foam-flakes of
the Northern Ocean driving through its streets,
and with the skeleton of its antique magnifi-
cence lifting up its gaunt arms into the sky.
One is of the Sea; one of the Cathedral—each
a mighty voice—the voice of a potent past;
the voice of an invigorating future.'

These be competent witnesses; and even
that prejudiced critic Samuel Johnson, who
came here in 1773 and demeaned himself
among the doctors and professors like a
whale among minnows—who summed up the
St Andrews streets as marked by 'the silence
and solitude of inactive indigence and gloomy
depopulation,' and saw nothing noteworthy

about St Rule's—yielded reluctantly at last to the charm of the place, and 'praised it with faint damns.'

The turrets of the eastern gable of the Cathedral are pricked up, at the farther end of the North Street vista, like two expectant ears. We have already approached this ancient fabric from several sides, and peeped at it from different points of view. It is time to make closer acquaintance ; and, resisting the temptation to follow the Butts Wynd to the Scores and the Links, and postponing also the invitation of Castle Street to explore the scarcely less renowned 'Arx Episcopi,' we enter the Cathedral precincts by the gate beside the Memorial Cross, which records the names of the 185 men of St Andrews who went into the Great War and came not back. They are but a handful compared to the exceeding great multitude who rest within and around the broken walls of the Cathedral, with the tall, battlemented and loopholed walls of Prior Hepburn as shelter from the tempest, and with the sea trampling on the shore beneath as their lullaby. Among the names in the Old and New Burying-grounds are some of the most revered and renowned in Scottish learning, art and science ; famous divines—who have a 'Sacred Ground' of their own—and men great in law, medicine, letters, war, business, and golf, all of them more or less closely associated with

F.F.　　　　　St Mary's College, St Andrews.

the credit and the fame of St Andrews, its University and its Links.

But the names of most of the sleepers around the Tower of St Rule and the fragments of the Cathedral of St Andrew are unknown, and even the bones found in the three stone coffins behind the high altar, and in the other five sarcophagi that lie exposed in the north transept, are matter of conjecture. They may be those of magnificent and munificent bishops and archbishops who helped to rear this fane —of Gammeline, Lamberton, and Trail; of Shevez, James Beaton, and, as a cloven skull may testify, Alexander Stewart, the 'Young Marcellus of his age,' son of a King, and pupil of Erasmus; or, more likely, they may not.

Utterly unknown are the owners of the confused mass of bones found within the 'Haunted Tower'; and, if possible, even more unassignable as to date and origin are the wonderfully rich collection of 'Celtic monuments'—including scores of fragments of crosses and graveslabs, covered, many of them, with intricate and artistic fretwork, and other ornament—that have been gathered into the Cathedral Museum, in a chamber adjoining the Chapter House. Many of them have been disinterred from graves in the Burying-ground, and some have been picked out the Prior's Wall, or from the foundations of the Cathedral itself, which, therefore, these stones doubtless long antedate. Hardly less worthy of note are the elaborately carved and moulded mediæval and later monuments, the impresses of personal and diocesan seals, the fragments of stained glass, from the Cathedral and St Mary's on the Kirkheugh, and the other antiquities that have found housing and arrangement in a repository that must be visited and studied if the early chapters of the history of the Cathedral Church are to be read aright.

It is a structure that is, perhaps, more impressive in its utter ruin than ever it was in the palmy days of its power and splendour, when it was the centre of the ecclesiastical life of Scotland. It is 'the wreck of a wreck,' of which little more remains than the eastern gable of the choir, or Lady Chapel ; a part, including the doorway, of the western front; the south wall of the nave and portions of the adjoining north transept and Chapter-House, and the foundations of some of the pillars of the aisles and of the central tower. Its comparative narrowness may have helped to give rise to the belief once current that it was 'the longest cathedral in Europe.' In reality it measures only 350 feet in length within the walls; so it is far out of competition even restricted to our island. But discoveries made within the present century indicate that if the building was not longer than it is at present, it was intended to be, by at least two bays ; and that it is probable that when Bishop Wishart, in 1273–79, 'sumptuously

re-edified' the west part of the Church, after it
had been destroyed by a storm, he built the
front in the present position, leaving outside of
it the narthex or Galilee of the original plan.

From its foundation in about 1160, by Bishop
Arnold, in the reign of Malcolm the Maiden,
it took some two centuries and a half in building. It was completed in time for the cele-
bration in it, by King Robert the Bruce, of
the recovery of Scottish Independence, a work
in which the patriotic Bishop Lamberton had
so mightily assisted; and it was consecrated
with great pomp in 1318 as 'a trophy and
memorial of Bannockburn.' There was another
great day in the Cathedral Church, when, in
1471, in the time of Bishop Graham, half-
brother and successor to the exemplary Bishop
Kennedy, there arrived the Papal Bulls, erecting
St Andrews into an archiepiscopal see, and finally
disposing of the claims of authority and super-
vision put forward on behalf of York.

The diocese at one time extended from the
Tweed tc the Dee; its Archbishops were Lords,
spiritual and temporal, who took precedence of
all the nobles and held rank after royalty. But
the time of downfall was not far off, and on the
11th of June 1559 came that thunderclap from
its humble neighbour the Town Kirk, which
toppled over the proud towers of the Cathedral.
'The Proveist, magistrates, and commonalty' of
the long subject burgh—including those whom

Knox himself called 'the rascal multitude'—set about pulling down 'the monuments of idolatry,' and they carried out their work 'with expedition,' and not with conspicuous gentleness or discrimination. Much has been irretrievably lost that all but zealots would have fain seen preserved; but so far as the buildings are concerned, they owe their demolition not so much to blind religious rancour, as to neglect and decay, to ill-directed greed and thrift. The holy and beautiful house in which their fathers worshipped became a quarry of stones for the inhabitants. In the seventeenth century one of the western pinnacles fell, narrowly missing a funeral party which had just entered through the gateway. Its later record is that of the preservation of the meagre remains that time and the hand of the destroyer have left.

In the attitude of a spectator or guardian, rather than as part of the ruins scattered around it, stands the Tower of St Rule, the 'mascotte' and symbol of their city to all true sons of St Andrews. Although it has lost the nave originally attached to it—on the evidence afforded by its western wall—and although of the balancing choir there is little else than a stump, this sturdy relic of the past, set four-square in the front of the seaward defences of town and temple, seems to rise serenely superior to the assaults of time and weather. Its date, its plan, and its purposes are enigmas on the

answers to which archæologists are not agreed.
But there is at least plausibility in the assump-
tion that it is the bell-tower of the basilica
which Bishop Robert, the founder of the Abbey,
raised in the first half of the twelfth century,
and thus the predecessor by a generation of
the Cathedral which rose hard by, and from
which, after the passing of eight hundred years,
it still seems to stand aloof.

The Tower of St Regulus is old, but hardly
old enough to have looked down on the
marriage procession of Malcolm and Margaret
when they came here to have their nuptials
celebrated by Turgot. Those who climb, mostly
in darkness, its 150 steps, and look abroad
from a height of 110 feet above the level
of the graves below, may be promised their
reward. All St Andrews, and the coasts and
suburbs thereof, lie at their feet ; looking
abroad, the prospect embraces a moiety of Fife
and a goodly slice of the fringes of Angus, as
far to the north as the Red Head of Lunan ;
under a favourable sky there may be descried
the outlines of the Grampians behind the range
of the Sidlaws, and, far out at sea, the Bell
Rock.

There are some who may feel content to take
the view from the crown of St Rule, like the
antiquity of the monument itself, for granted.
Of such was Walter Scott, when he paid his
last visit to St Andrews. He resignedly accepted

his disinclination to climb again to the summit
of the Tower as 'the first decided acquiescence
in the lot of old age,' and in his 'Journal' he
records, with a pang, how, 'thirty-four years
earlier, he had carved a name, in runic characters,
on the turf beside the Castle Gate.'

To the Castle Gate we repair, first taking a
peep through a crevice in the wall of the Chapter-
House of the Cathedral into the cloisters of the
Abbey ruins, to which as yet the public have
no right of entry. Much work was done by the
fifth Marquis of Bute, the owner of the Abbey
grounds, in laying bare the foundations, and in
revealing the positions, and, as far as possible,
restoring the forms, of the Refectory and
Fratery, the cellars, and other parts of the
monastic buildings, including the old Guest
House, to which James the Sixth fled, 'like
a bird out of the fowler's snare,' for solace-
ment and shelter after the Raid of Ruthven.

It is a page out of the St Andrews past that
is as yet half turned down. The site of the
Castle looks, on the other hand, like a page
that had been rudely torn out. The fortunes of
the Bishop's Palace, whose appearance, like its
experiences, was much more that of a feudal
stronghold than of an episcopal residence, have
been closely bound by fate and circumstances
to those of the Cathedral; they rose and they
fell together. Not a stone can now be pointed
out of the structure raised by Bishop Roger

about the year 1200, on the rock-bound margin
of the sea which keeps constantly eating at its
foundations. After having been razed 'to the
yerd' in the English Wars, it was entirely rebuilt
in 1401 by Bishop Trail, who may have added,
or may only have inherited, that notorious
appendage to the Sea Tower, the gruesome

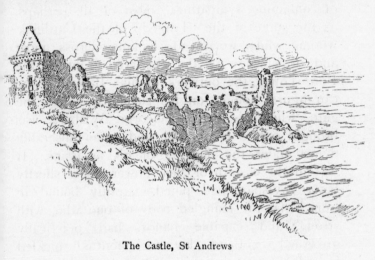

The Castle, St Andrews

'Bottle Dungeon,' in which, as legend will have
it, the young Duke of Rothesay, heir to the
Crown, was confined, before removal, for more
effectual disposal, to Falkland. James II. of
Scots occupied, and the ill-fated James III. was
born in, St Andrews Castle. Later it became
centre and guerdon of assaults and defences in
which archbishops were alternately besieged and
besiegers. The Reformation quarrel was fiercely

'fought to a finish' at the gate and within the walls which Archbishop Hamilton had newly re-erected, and on which David Beaton was engaged in putting the finishing touches when Norman Leslie and his ruthless company burst through and slew him.

It is a fabric fraught with scenes of violence, of conflicting sympathies; most of all, perhaps, as the stage of the 'Tragedy of the Cardinal,' whom, while we stand, looking across moat and drawbridge to the shattered front of the Fore Tower, the outwork of his 'Babylon,' one can figure 'lolling on his cushions,' above the gate, while his enemy, George Wishart, was brought out to be burned, and again miserably dying under the daggers of his assassins. It was in the eastern or Sea Tower where shortly before Wishart had pined, 'straitly bound in irons,' that the mangled body of one who, with strong and capable hands, had practically governed Scotland, lay for months 'pickled in salt,' and 'closit in a kiste.' Even those who think that 'the loon was well away,' have to acknowledge, with Sir David Lyndesay, that 'the deed was foully done.'

The Castle had to suffer other shocks of outrageous fortune, and to undergo later re-edifyings, before being suffered to fall into its present state of utter collapse and decay. As we climb about its broken walls and stairways, look out of its empty windows, saunter on the sward around the draw-well in its courtyard, or peer down into the orifice whence a subterranean passage—relic, it is thought, of sixteenth century mining or countermining—has been found extending to below a house in the adjoining Castle Street, we feel the air of this ancient stronghold of proud and aspiring prelates to be, if exceedingly peaceful, exceedingly dolorous. But one can see also that it is being carefully and sympathetically tended in its days of decline. As the result of intelligent excavation and study, its story is being slowly but surely read in its stones, although the heraldic arms over the entrance are too worn by weather and ill usage to reveal whether they are those of Beaton or of that other masterful builder, Archbishop Hamilton.

More cheerful on the whole, though not less suggestive, are the aspects and associations of its surroundings, although these include, outside of the north wall of the Cathedral, the spot, almost overhead St Rule's Cave in the sea cliff, where the aged Walter Myln, the last of the 'Protestant Martyrs,' was burned at the stake. The 'Martyrs' Monument,' which records along with Myln and Wishart, the names of Patrick Hamilton and Henry Forrest, is depressing and heavy in its appeal to the eye and to the memory, as perhaps it was designed to be. Beside it are the Bow Butts and the 'Witches Hill,' and, on the shore below, the

'Witches Lake,' by a happy stroke of modern sorcery converted into a Ladies' Bathing Pond.

Close by, and well apart from the shading trees and stately mansions and hotels of the Scores, stands the Clubhouse of the 'Royal and Ancient,' fronting its subject Links—the revered 'Mecca of Golf,' where the laws of the game are written and expounded, and many of the oldest and greatest of its achievements have been chronicled. In its presence, and with the rolling expanse of greensward, pitted with bunkers and fringed by sand-dunes, spreading before us until it meets the tidewater of the Eden, it becomes impossible for a time to think or to speak of anything other than Golf—its hazards and delights, its glorious uncertainties, its unaccountable disappointments, its problems, profound and intricate as those of the Sphinx. It is an absorption that endures even when the West Sands are basking in the sunshine that flashes from the lines of breakers rolling in with the tide, and when the footpaths that wind among benty hills are painted yellow with the bloom of the whin and the rock-rose.

In St Andrews, as was written nearly a century ago, golf is not a mere pastime, but 'a business and a passion'; here men not only golf to live, but live to golf. 'They begin to play in the morning, and stop only for dinner'—the early dinner now called lunch—'and after practising in the sea breezes all day, they discuss it all night.

The original large allowance of golfing ground
has been multiplied three or fourfold—taking
no account of 'Putting Greens'—since the New,
the Jubilee, and the Eden courses have been
added to the Old Course. Each is beginning to
rival, in quality and reputation, the links on
which 'Old Tom' and 'Young Tommy' Morris,
Allan Robertson, the Kirkcaldys, and other
Heroes of the Game of former days, too
numerous to have their names recounted here,
won their fame. To follow any of them is
to pursue the 'fleein' ba'' far out towards
some 'Point Turn-again' in the vicinity of the
Eden estuary, where the sheaf of towers of the
'haunted town' of St Andrews becomes a distant
and fading vision.

With many a look back towards the City of
Enchantment, we leave turf for highway, and
pursue our path towards Guard Bridge, Leuchars
and Tents Moor.

LEUCHARS AND TENTS MOOR.

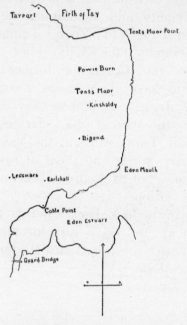

Oh, the dreary, dreary moorland!
Oh, the barren, barren shore!

Locksley Hall.

IMPRESSIONS of the way to Leuchars and
to the regions beyond Eden must vary
greatly with the weather, the time of the year,
and, most of all, the state of the tide. They
may be cheerful and inspiring in bright sunshine
and with a heaving and dimpling flood of sea-

water filling the whole space, a mile and more in breadth, between us and the sand-dunes of Tents Moor. They can be depressing enough under a heavy sky and at half-tide, when sand-banks and mud-banks, and stretches of black mussel scaup and dull-coloured sea-marsh, rise out of the shallow waters that were once the port of St Andrews, and fill nearly the whole space from shore to shore.

There is drier and firmer ground as the estuary narrows, as the salty sea-meadows turn to grass fields, and as the hills of Logie—Lucklaw, Ardit, Craigfoodie, Craiglug, Craigsanquhar, and the rest—draw nearer, and the big bulk and quaint steeple of Leuchars Kirk loom above the horizon line. The presence of the latest and strangest of human inventions is declared in the brand-new buildings of the Aerodrome, set against the woods that surround the ancient House of Earlshall. Overhead there hovers and buzzes something that looks not so much like a monstrous bird of the air as a stupendous dragon-fly, but swifter and more powerful than any Roc of Eastern fable. We cannot call upon its aid to cross the gulf, and no coble waits in these days at the constriction at Coble Shore. We must e'en go round by Guard Bridge, and cross, as previous wayfarers have done for full five hundred years, by Bishop Wardlaw's Bridge.

Guard Bridge has been during all these centuries a place of some note, and, within reasonable

degrees, of some trade; and it alters compara-
tively little, except to change its chief industry
with the times. It has done business in the past
in distilling and other trades; it is at present

Guard Bridge.

mainly interested, as its cluster of chimney stalks
declare, in paper-making; and it has lately
tacked on to itself a model Airmen's Village.
Its industrial and strategic value rests upon the
fact that it is at the head of the tide water, where

both the river Eden and the Moultrie Burn enter the salt flats, and form, as it were, covering moats of observation and protection against those approaching St Andrews, with innocent or evil intent, from the west and north. This, no doubt, the good Bishop perceived when he built his famous six-arched bridge, which bears a shield of arms and a pastoral staff inscribed on one of its keystones.

Though narrow, according to modern ideas— for two motor-cars can with difficulty squeeze past each other on its highway, and the embayments provided for the ancient foot passenger are still a life-saving need for his present-day successor—it is still the main means of transit (apart from the railway) between Leuchars and St Andrews. It is said that people are yet alive, or are not long dead, who remember when the Guard Bridge was secured by a chain that forbade all but four-wheeled chariots to make use of it, so that humbler vehicles were compelled to wait the ebb-tide and ' take to the water.'

Truly St Andrews and its dependencies owed much to, if they suffered much from, their episcopal superiors. Only a couple of miles upstream is another bridge, built some two centuries later by another Lord Spiritual, Archbishop Spottiswoode for the service of the public, as well as for con veniency of access to his Castle or Palace of Dairsie—set over against the entrance to Dura Den—wherein he is said to have written his

Church history and superintended the erection of Dairsie Kirk, built in a nondescript style of Gothic, as model, which, sooth to say, none of them have followed, for all Parish Kirks in Scotland.

No one can say who was designer and builder of the old Church of Leuchars—any more than it can be told who founded the Castle, with which,

Site of Leuchars Castle.

doubtless, it was at one time in close relationship. They occupy mounds, some half a mile apart, each dominating the village and a subject territory once extending from the Eden to the Tay. But while the Church continues to rear above the plain its massive bulk, the Castle has been bloated out of existence, and is represented only by an oval tumulus, rising out of what was once a marsh, surrounded by a moat, and now crested by a convocation of aged and twisted yews, and watched over, from the neighbouring

F.F.

Earlshall.

14

farm of Castleton, by a picturesque old dovecot
with corbelled corners. It is one of the many
traditional strongholds of the 'Thane of Fife'
to be found along the coasts and in the interior
of the Kingdom ; and probably it had not got
beyond the primitive 'mote-and-bailey' stage
when Pembroke's English troops seized and
destroyed it in 1327. Late in the twelfth century
it was in the supposedly Celtic hands of Nes of
Locres, from whom it passed by marriage of his
heiress to the powerful family of the De Quincis,
Earls of Winchester, after whom the lands came
into possession of Lindsays, Carnegies, and other
owners.

It may have been Nes, or a predecessor of his
line, who reared the little gem of Norman architecture, the most ornate specimen surviving in
the land, which some time before 1187 he gave
over to the Augustinian Canons of St Andrews.
By good fortune the double tiers of its chevroned,
pillared, and arcaded apse and chancel, its richly
moulded groinings, and its caps and cornicings
embellished with grotesque heads and floral
ornament, have survived many a storm. The
worst mischance that has befallen these grey old
sculptured walls is, not that they are partly sunk
among the gravestones and the mould of mortality
that beset them, but that they have had attached
to them later additions that overshadow them
in bulk and are incongruous in style. Of Leuchars
Kirk it may be said that, from east to west, it

increases in height and size, and diminishes still more rapidly in age and interest. Even the seventeenth century belfry, although it has merits

Leuchars Church.

of its own, is out of keeping with the more ancient building below, the roof and part of the groining of which were removed to make place for it.

There are incongruities in the story of Leuchars Church as in its architecture. Alexander Henderson—the 'Knox of the Second Reformation'—was its pastor for over twenty years in the early part of the seventeenth century. He came as a protégé of that much-hated and vilified Archbishop Gledstanes, and was fain to get entry to his fold 'through a window.' Then he heard a sermon preached at Forgan, by that stout opponent of Prelacy, Robert Bruce, from the text, 'He that entereth not in by the door, the same is a thief and a robber'; and altering his views and his rule of faith, he lived to become the champion of Presbyterianism in Fife and in London, and joint framer of the National Covenant.

Close by Leuchars Castle is the House of Pitlethie, to the predecessor of which, it is said, James VI. was wont to come for hunting and retirement, in witness whereof there is pointed out a stone bearing the Royal arms built into a wall. The name of the 'Earl's Hall' has, however, moved a mile away and, with a goodly store of ancient heirlooms and traditions clinging about it, has taken shelter in the woods, looking down upon Guard Bridge and the tide of the Eden, that have long surrounded the home of a branch of the family of the Bruces of Clackmannan, whose immediate predecessors were Monypennys of Pitmilly.

Earlshall makes ceremonious announcement of

itself as by seneshal and trumpeter—first by a
lordly Gatehouse, which, though of late date,
has toned and weathered into an aspect of age
as well as dignity, and then by a dovecot standing forth behind a paved terrace, like a pert
and diminutive squire proclaiming, through the
chanticleer on its ridge, the glories of the
baronial house.

Like a chateau out of some volume of romance
is this stately sixteenth-century mansion, ruddy
of aspect, except where draped with ivy and
other evergreens, flanked by towers, and crowned
above its three massive storeys by gables,
corbels, and attic windows. Over the great
gateway in the curtain-wall is a panel with
the arms and initials of the builder, Sir William
Bruce ; and other inscriptions plentifully sprinkled
over lintels and dormers, as on mantels and walls
within, make known to all comers that it was
erected by this Lord of Earlshall in 1546, and
was completed by his grandson of the same
name in 1607, and record, also, the alliances
of these and of later owners with Lyndesays,
Meldrums, and other families of note.

On entering the portal into the courtyard
beyond, and passing its sculptured draw-well
and the doorway in the roundel tower in the
re-entering angle of the main building, from
which the great staircase winds all the way up
to its platformed and parapeted roof, and then
descending into the walled garden, curiously and

lavishly decorated with examples of the 'topiary art' in clipped yew and box, the house is found

The Gatehouse, Earlshall.

to take on an aspect yet more romantic and impressive. The most noteworthy of its adorn-

ments are, however, within, and not chiefly in
the hall over the vaulted ground floor, with
its spacious fireplace bearing the arms and
initials of Alexander Bruce and Elizabeth Leslie,
but in the ' Painted Gallery ' extending throughout the second floor. Here is a ' Chamber of
Imageries,' full fifty feet in length, on which has
been depicted, in black and white, what has been
called 'a treatise on Scottish Heraldry,' in the
shape of the armorials and mottoes of the leading Fife and other houses of the time, along
with a selection of those of sundry Kings and
potentates of foreign countries or drawn from
classical or Scripture history. These are on
round panels, and interspersed with them and
with proverbs, maxims and moral apothegms,
in Roman characters, we find a menagerie of
strange and selcouth beasts, real and imaginary,
as they were known to the natural history of the
period—Lion and Bear with Sphinx and Hydra,
and including a ' Svyn Baib,' which may be translated Sow and Piglet.

Many of these pictured devices, painted on
wood on the flat arch of the roof, became
undecipherable during the seventy years that
Earlshall lay neglected and untenanted. So
far as was found possible the panels have been
restored, like other features of the building, by
the late owner, Mr Thomas Mackenzie, but a
number are left blank. In new hands the place
has again the prospect of careful keeping.

The mottoes, like those in the dismal and deserted 'Palace' at Culross, are such as one can profitably con and carry away, in spite of difficulties over lettering and spelling. Some are quaint, caustic and familiar, like—

> 'A nyce Wife and a backdoor,
> Maketh the rich man poore.'

Or this exhortation to charity :

> 'Denye nane of them al
> For little thou knowest herein this Lyf
> Quhat chaunce may befall.'

Either, or both, of these sayings may have been exemplified in the lives of the Ladies of Earlshall whose initials and armorials are generously distributed over the outer and inner walls of the dwelling they graced—by ' E. L., Elizabeth Leslie, wife of the builder, for example ; or by ' M. M.,' Margaret Meldrum, of Seggie, spouse of his grandson and successor in the lands and in the task of construction. As to ' D. A. L.,' Dame Agnes Lyndesay, lady of a William Bruce of Earlshall, who flourished in 1620, we hear of her on a grave slab in Leuchars Churchyard, which attests that ' in her life she was charitable to the poore and profitable to that House,' and having 'dyed 1635, of her age 68,' she 'waiteth in hope.'

In the popular memory of 'that House' of the Bruces—who dropped out of possession later than the profitable Agnes's time—all that

lingers are the harsh and evil deeds of the
Bruce of Earlshall who was the zealous per-
secutor of the Covenanters, the 'Colloguer' with
Claverhouse and Dalyell of Binns, who turned
the tide of battle at Airds Moss, and hunted
to the death, in Fife and elsewhere, the 'Men
of the Moss Haggs.'

Beyond Earlshall and Comerton farm, and
out of a dark little plantation of pines, one
comes suddenly forth on Tents Moor, a waste
and empty territory, a Land of Lost Footsteps,
across which there is scarcely the track of
wheels, that occupies the north-eastern corner
of Fife.   Bounded by three seas, the Eden
Estuary, the North Sea, and the Firth of
Tay, it has no definite frontier on the land
side, where moor merges into cultivated land.
Woods, mostly of old firs, intrude on it, and
the Forestry Commission have seized upon its
northern parts, where doubtless it will be
changed beyond recognition before many years
are past.   But in the meantime no one can
enter it without feeling that he has penetrated
into a region apart, and, as it were, enchanted,
so solitary is it, and yet so spacious, so free
to, and so full of, the elemental spirits of
the sea and of the air, of the level moorland
and the rolling sandhills.

From the shores of its tidal waters, St
Andrews looks, in different lights, now close
at hand, now unattainably remote.   It has

been fantastically suggested that Tents Moor
has been reserved as the Happy Hunting
Grounds of the disembodied spirits of departed
golfers. From these Elysian fields beyond
Eden they have ample space and verge
enough to play themselves, and to watch the
living at their play. If you seat yourself on
one of the grassy mounds or sandy hillocks
that fringe the estuary, and look southward,
you become aware, in clear weather, of tiny
objects moving, with a certain appearance of
order and purpose towards you, or away from
you, on the tumbled green mounds beyond
the river. Some are clad in grey or black,
like ants, and a few are bright red, like lady-
birds; and if you watch them narrowly you
will note that individuals among them dis-
appear for a space as if into the bowels of
the earth, while from the spot fancy sees up-
rising a faint cloud of sand, the token of toil
and disaster and anguished objurgation. These
are, of course, the golfers on the St Andrews
Links, and behind them, shining in the level
light, or glooming under the shadow of the
high land behind, are the towers and spires
of the venerable Cathedral City, and outside
the pure blue spaces of ocean, whose sound
and breath pervade all the coasts and recesses
of Tents Moor.

But when out of the sea steals a mist and
wipes out the vision, it is difficult to believe

that necromancy is not at work.   It is 'a pleasing and plausible fancy' that the mighty heroes of the prehistoric and historic ages of golf have flitted no farther than across the river, and that 'from coigns of vantage on the sandhills of the moor they watch the fortunes of the game on their beloved links, applauding some well-judged piece of play with niblick or putter, or wagging the head disapprovingly over modern changes in the sport.   One can imagine them in the gloaming, or even in broad daylight, driving shadowy balls and holing long putts in the secluded hollows of Tents Moor.   For there are none to overlook these ghostly gamesters at their sport'; and there is room for a dozen or a score of courses between the Earlshall woods and the point, opposite to Abertay Sands, that marks the entrance to the Firth of Tay.

Like nature, however, man abhors a vacuum, and these empty and breezy spaces, bordered all round by sandy beach and carpeted by turf, cannot be expected to remain much longer un-occupied, except by the rabbits and moles and by the whaups and other wild fowl.   For here is ideal ground for a settlement devoted to golf and sea-bathing.   Soil and sward do not greatly differ from those of the 'Home of Golf' on the south side of the Eden.   Along the sea margin runs a like range of sand-dunes, peaked or table-topped, and tufted with bent—terrible places for a ball to go astray in.   But in the lee of this barrier there are good sound turf and rowth of hazards; and you can drive and follow your ball—no doubt with many strange and perilous adventures—for miles in the direction of Tayport, until brought up by the growing plantations beyond the Powie burn.

On the land side of the dunes, the route— marked chiefly by footways to some salmon-fisher's shelter by the shore, or to an upturned boat, where temporary shelter can be had in a rainstorm—is in places fearfully and wonder-fully bordered by great strips of ling and of tussocky grass, of the kind that would soon be blasted off the face of the earth had golfers' curses the power to kill. The moor is crossed also by deep ditches, known as 'canals,' that have been cut in parallel straight lines for drainage purposes, and that require, like the fences of barbed wire, to be negotiated with caution.

Several of these obstacles we had to clear, in making for the white chimney of Bigend, a solitary cottage, a mile away from anywhere, that rises above a clump of shrubs shading a pool in which lint and hemp used to be steeped. For the moor was not always so uninhabited as it is to-day; and a group of wind-battered plane-trees, skirmishers of the Fir Park Wood, mark the site of an extinct weaving hamlet, the very name of which is forgotten.

Traces of Danish speech and customs, it is

said, still linger round the verges of Tents Moor
—'Sheughy Dyke' is said to be an older name—
which, tradition asserts, was at one time settled
by a company of sturdy Scandinavian stock.
There are legends that smuggling, poaching, and
wrecking, were the chief industries of this No
Man's Land set on a shore that looks across
the North Sea towards Jutland. The kind
people at Bigend told us that only a few years
since there died an old man, whose name was
Linnæus—or Linny—Simpson, who claimed that
he was of this Danish descent, and who told
of an ancestor, living near by, who, suspecting
one of his neighbours of stealing, lay down to
watch beside the hemp, with a sharp axe ready
to smite. By and by a hand and arm were
seen stealing over the hemp; and down came
the axe, and off came the hand. Shortly afterwards the neighbour appeared out of doors,
minus a hand. 'He said naething o' his han',
and the owner said naething o' his exe.'

Gipsies were wont to camp on the moor, and
their wandering tents are even thought to have
given it its name. These grassy mounds and
sandy hollows in the lee of the Kinshaldy Woods,
where foreign coins are still occasionally picked
up, might tell strange stories of wreck and
plunder. One, not quite forgotten, is of a
French ship, laden with wines, that drifted
ashore on this inhospitable coast. The parishes
of Leuchars and Ferry-Port-on-Craig were, it

is said, drenched for months with claret and cognac; and part of the spoil is still hidden in the Moor, perhaps to be disinterred some day from a bunker with a sand iron.

The tradition of Danish settlement and encampment is pervasive and tenacious in Northern Fife. It is discussed by Dr Wm. Brown, Professor of Church History in St Andrews, in an article to the *Archæologia Scotica*, which describes a visit paid to 'Sheughy Dyke' in August 1822. It is right to say that he found 'no Danes left' on the Moor at that date; the last had been a family of 'Landsmans'; although words survived, like 'tafel' for 'table,' apparently imported from across the North Sea. The story ran that the Scots, 'rallied by a predecessor of Hay of Newton,' on the edge of the moor—the same tale is told of Luncarty, of Naughton, of Inverdovat and other places on the supposed line of retreat, and always with the name of Hay attached—drove the invaders before them, until they finally found shelter behind the entrenchments they had formed in Sheughy Dyke, 'near the centre of which, at Kingshaldrie' (Kinshaldy) 'the tent of the King of the Danes was pitched'—hence the name. The lochs and dykes of the region are remains of the Danish entrenchments; or so he may believe who lists.

There can be few places for the quiet, con-

centrated study of nature like Tents Moor.
It is a favourite resort and resting-place of
the many species of resident birds and of
migrants that make their first land-fall from
the East in this sanctuary. Pallas's Sand
Grouse came hither in great numbers from
their Siberian home during the great exodus
of 1888, and for years afterwards made regular
settlement here. Kestrel hawks nest in the
Fir Park Wood, and for a time there was the
nucleus there of a heronry. As the late Dr
John H. Wilson tells us in his 'Nature Study
Rambles,' the eider duck is a regular nesting
species; and one is never long out of sight
and earshot in spring, summer, and autumn, of
plover and curlew, sand-piper and oyster-catcher.
Nor are the botanical treasures of the locality
less rare and attractive; and nowhere surely
does the crimson and white bell heather grow
in richer profusion or more beautiful blooms.

There are also the treasures of the shore at
high-water or at low tide—mollusca and algæ
and other frequenters of salt water and sandy
beach. With these we are engaged when into
a little embayment of the coast-line sail a
family squadron of eider duck. The parents,
grey plumaged with white markings on their
wing-coverts, sail on in front with the young
broods in tow—little black handfuls of down
that take gallantly and buoyantly the billows
that come in, white-crested, from the open sea.

They have found their way to salt water through what to them must have seemed shaggy and endless forests of ling and bent, from their nests, perhaps a mile or more inland, and are now taking their first lessons in navigation.

Near the edge of the water is a mysterious white object that looks more mysterious still as we draw nearer. Is it a ball of wool, or a dead gull swept ashore by the waves? No; for it is standing on a substantial pair of black webbed feet. But then, again, it is without a head! In response to a poke from a walking-stick, a head, armed with a long, sharp, and scissors-like bill, surmounted by fierce, pale blue staring eyes, emerges suddenly from below a wing and makes a swift lounge at the disturbing agent. The owner gives no other indication of moving from the spot where it is enjoying its siesta, and we leave the irate gannet alone in its glory, sole monarch of the sea-shore within sight.

Moor and sands are not, however, so destitute of occupation and of the resources of civilisation as one might deem; for in the hollow of the Powie burn, beside a cottage at the tail of the Kinshaldy Woods, we come unexpectedly upon a couple of motor-cars, a pleasure-yacht sheltering in the tidal creek, and a group of young men and maidens basking in the sun or paddling in the stream.

To extend the exploration of Tents Moor, in the line of the two white lighthouses that mark the entrance to the navigable channel of the Tay, all the way to Tents Point, seems, under the hot sun, needless waste of time and energy. So bearings are taken for Ferry-Port-on-Craig —delightful name, once corrupted to 'Partan Craig,' and now abbreviated and rendered less expressive as Tayport—by cutting across newly afforested ground to a deserted farm-stead at the corner of the Fettersloch Wood, and then through the Morton Links and past the new small holdings and cottages at Garpit. And so, by Cannieport and the golf-course, and the big spinning and weaving mill that represents the chief industry of the place, to the shore of the Firth and to the Kirk and the harbour of the old Ferry Port on the Craig.

F.F.   Tay Bridge, from Balmerino.

THE FERRIES ON TAY.

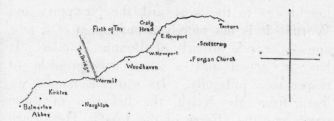

> A Chieftain to the Highlands boun',
> Cried, 'Boatman, do not tarry,
> And I'll gie thee a sillar poun',
> To row me o'er the Ferry.'
>
> *Lord Ullin's Daughter.*

AT the beginning of Tayport—so let the place be called, since its inhabitants appear to wish it—we are, in reality, at the beginnings of Dundee. We have fairly turned our backs on the South and are facing the North. Airs and legends are wafted not only from the sea, but from the Highlands—from Northern Pictland, whose outer line of defence, the Sidlaws, behind the great ditch of the Firth, keeps in sight all the rest of the way, as, for the most part, does the smoke, if not also the chimney-stalks and houses, of what its citizens sometimes call 'Juteopolis.' Dundee, with the aid of the Tay Bridge, has stretched its filaments across what in old times was called 'Dundee Water,' and, by right of colonisation and exploitation, has annexed the 'Waterside' of Fife.

Tayport has not, however, yielded wholly to the needs and tastes of the settlers and summer visitors from the Angus shore. Unlike its neighbours to the westward, the Newports and Wormit, it is not merely a mushroom of a new age—a seaside suburb of Bonnie Dundee. It has an actual and a legendary chronicle of respectable antiquity. Its earliest name, we learn from Mr Neish, the historian of these parts, was the 'Ferry of the Loaf.' Here once more we are on the trail of Macduff, fleeing across salt water with enemies on his track— going farther to fare worse perhaps, since partisans of Macbeth may be waiting for him about Glamis, or lurking in the passes near Dunsinane. He had not on him, says the story, a 'sillar pound,' or its equivalent as passage money, and the hard-hearted ferryman exacted, as recompense for the crossing, the loaf of bread with which the sore-pressed Thane hoped to sustain life on the hostile northern shore.

There have been many squabblings and chafferings over fares and the like since then. For the Tay boatmen had at one time the reputation of being both grasping and ill-tongued. Much history passed northward and southward by way of the Port on the Craig and of Broughty, in the persons, among others,

of Covenanters in flight or pursuit; of Rob
Roy and other invaders or refugees in the
Jacobite Rebellions, and of passengers in the
later times of the French Wars and the stage
coaches. The traffic across the water is no
longer of the old volume, or conducted by the
old methods and by the old type of men and
boats.

Tayport conserves, however, some relics of the
past; and a flavour of the elder age may be
caught by those who wander about its church
and harbour, and the neighbouring streets and
rocks. Its houses are mostly one-storeyed, and
many of them, in the narrower streets, are roofed
with tiles. The 'Castle,' in which some have
detected the traces of a Pictish 'broch,' while
others have relegated it to a comparatively late
period of defensive work, has disappeared in
almost all but name. The Parish Church sticks
to the breast of the brae, surrounded by gravestones that record many tragedies by sea and
land, among them the sinking of the steamer
Dalhousie on Abertay Sands, in a night of
storm in the winter of 1864, with all her crew
and passengers, of whom only the bodies of a
few came to land, and were committed to the
earth beside the Kirk, or in the 'Strangers'
Ground' adjacent.

The building was erected, or re-erected, little
more than a century ago by the Rev. Dr Robert
Dalgleish, who, besides being minister of the

parish, of which he wrote a description in the
' Old Statistical Account,' was Laird of Scotscraig,
and thus proprietor of all the land about Tayport, and founder besides, under the name of
Maryton, of the adjacent East Newport. Scotscraig dominates from its heights, and from the
midst of its woods, this part of Fife. It took
its name from an early possessor, a descendant
of the Wizard, Michael Scot of Balwearie, to
distinguish it from the other ' Craigs ' that abound
in the region. Its most intimate associations,
however, are with Archbishop James Sharp, to
whom, and to his son, Sir William, after him,
it belonged during a considerable tract of the
seventeenth century, and who began and carried
out many improvements, including the building
of a mansion of which some remains are extant
in the old walled garden, including a gateway
bearing in the centre of the arch 'a sculptured
stone showing a mitre and star, with the initials
A. J. S. and the date 1667.'

On an outer gateway the date ' 1680 ' has
been read, the year after the murder of the
Archbishop ; it looks as much like ' 1630.'
There are an ancient sun-dial and dovecot, but
of the venerable sycamore—the ' Bell Tree '—
from which the servants of His Grace were
summoned to their meals, no trace is left, and
the like has happened to a still more famous
patriarch among Fife walnut-trees, which was
blown down, it is said, by the same wild blast

that overthrew the Tay Bridge on the night of the 28th December 1879.

From his doorstep the Archbishop could look abroad, as we did, over a wide expanse of sea and land—over the whole level spread of Tents Moor, to the towers of St Andrews and to the hills behind, so intertwined with his fate. There are still fine trees left in Scotscraig, in spite of the fresh ravages wrought among them by the January gale of 1927. It is indeed, as has been claimed, 'one of the most romantic and beautiful of country seats in the north of Fife,' abounding, besides woods and lawns, in sheltered valleys and craggy heights, on one of which is perched a 'Waterloo Tower.' It seems a pity that the Dundee Corporation, who were at one time in possession, should have parted with it to private hands.

From the southern shoulder of Scotscraig, one can glimpse, crouching in a sequestered valley, the ivied walls of the old Kirk of Forgan and of the adjacent House of Kirkton, and between them the famous yew-trees, that are supposed to be the oldest living things in the Kingdom of Fife. Forgan parish comes down to the sea at Newport and Wormit; it is an important part of the Fringes, and it is worth while penetrating so far inland, if one follows a footpath that takes one by the ruined farmstead of Rosebery, on a hill near by which was fought the battle of Inverdovat, one of the obscure battles with the Danish pirates who made these shores too frequent a house of call, and then by—in this case into—the Manse of Forgan, aptly described in Robert Leighton's poem, 'The Baptisement of the Bairn,' as 'a cozie spot weel shoogit frae the breeze.'

Of Forgan Kirk, the original situation of which appears to have been an island in a marsh surrounded by hills, only the bare walls remain ; and these do not contradict, if they do not avouch, the claim that it as old as, if not older than, Leuchars, like which it was, from an early date, a Priory Church of St Andrews, and served by its canons. The grant was made in 1150 by Alan de Lascelles, a family that held the fortalice of Naughton before the Hays came to it. The name of St Phillan's, or St Fillan's, sometimes given to it, may imply a Celtic foundation. A less familiar Saint's name is that of St Fort—locally pronounced Sanford—bestowed on an estate, long in the possession of the Nairnes, who 'went out' in the '45 ; it is made familiar as that of the first halting-place on the Fife side of the Tay Bridge, by the through route of the London and North-Eastern Railway. Later owners, the Stewarts, are buried in Forgan Churchyard, as are the Berries of Tayfield, once Inverdovat, and the Gillespies of Kirkton, who abandoned their old mansion to decay when they moved to Mountquhannie.

Kirkton House, only a stone-throw away, is in a worse state of dilapidation than the Kirk. Between them stand the immemorial yews; but even these have yielded to the pressure of time and of the wind. One of the five fell in the January storm that wrought such havoc in Fife and all over Scotland; it lies prostrate and withered. Considering all that it saw and survived it deserves at least decent removal; without it its old companions, including a great walnut, continue to cast a melancholy depth of shade over a hallowed spot.

Old Forgan—or should it be Forgrund?—had its 'Loft,' for the 'Boatmen of the Waterside,' which was not reinstalled when the Church was, in 1841, removed a mile nearer to Newport. It testified that, in spite of their dubious reputation, the 'Folk of the Waterside' were not oblivious to spiritual things. Although they were occasionally brought before the Church Courts for Sabbath-breaking and other offences, their pastors are found making excuses for their too robust language and manners, and hinting that these had been corrupted by 'evil communications.' They were subject to 'temptation' through the conduct and example of 'strangers.' As the Reverend James Burn of Forgan wrote in 1795: 'Some of the ferry-men are sober and discreet; others of them borrow the language and behaviour of those who frequent the passage, especially of such whom they look on as their superiors in rank and station. How much it is to be regretted that from so many of these they often learn to be rude and profane!'

Even in those days, fully a century and a quarter ago, the Tay Ferries were suffering loss and change through the building of the bridge at Perth. Newport was in its infancy, with perhaps a hundred inhabitants; not until a generation or two later did it come into corporate existence. There were two competing ferries on the shore opposite to Dundee —Newport, formerly Seamylnes, which had been started by the Dundee Guildry so early as 1713, and Woodhaven, a mile farther west, Needless to relate the tale of their rivalries and vicissitudes. Newport, which had called itself 'New Dundee' and 'New Port of Dundee' before it settled down to its present name, was the ultimate winner. Its harbour was built in 1823; steam came in; Woodhaven was abandoned as a public ferry more than a hundred years ago; now it is represented by a little creek and pier, off which the 'Mars' Training Ship—once a fairlie now a landmark— has been stationed since 1869, and affords the main means and reason of its existence.

Yet Woodhaven has witnessed stirring times and perilous scenes, in the days when the fear of Bonaparte was in the land, the days before

railways, when as many as twenty-eight boats—
yawls or pinnaces—plied, without rule or system,
on the Tay Ferries, which, then among 'the
worst and most dangerous,' became afterwards
'the safest, most expeditious, and convenient
in the Kingdom'; and there was a babel of

Mars Training Ship, Woodhaven

confusion on the arrival or departure of every
stage-coach. Tom Hood, then a young journalist
living in Dundee, describes a thrilling scene in
1815, when a pinnace from the Dundee side,
overloaded with passengers bound to hear Dr
Thomas Chalmers preach at Kilmany, foundered
in a gust off Newport, taking down with her
twenty-two persons, including her commander,

that rough diamond, 'Cossack Jock' Spalding, or 'Ballad Jock,' from the ballads he wrote and sung in denouncement of 'Boney.'

As has been suggested, Newport is separated from Tayport by a good deal more than the two miles of road or rail between the towns. Although both are on the Waterside, and both are more or less offspring of the Ferries and dependent on Dundee, they virtually turn their backs on one another. One faces the north-east and the other the north-west, and their alignment expresses in a measure their attitude to each other. The old Ferry Port has still its hand in trade; the young rival that has out-stripped it in the race for wealth and population is devoted more to the housing and entertainment of what are, from the Fife point of view, Out-landers. It is a 'residential' town, which makes a good effect from the river, and from the opposite side of the Firth, by its long lines of villas ranged to advantage along the terraced slopes of its site, among trees and gardens, and is well provided with all the means, in new and sound condition, for improving the mind and passing the time pleasantly.

That is to say, there is little in it, east or west, to detain the traveller who is looking for what is antique and picturesque and char-acteristic of Fife. Better, except when one is in a hurry, and troubled with corns, it is to take the shore path from the lighthouse to the west of Tayport harbour, and follow it at least as far as the Craighead at the east end of Newport. This may involve some out-and-in and up-and-down scrambling. But there is always beside us the reward of the broad stream of the Firth, with its passing craft; beyond and in front the myriad works and habitations on the farther shore, crowned by the Law and its memorial pyramid, softened and made pictorial by distance; the huts and nets of the salmon fishers, who reap a rich harvest from this part of the river; and the children playing, or the lovers sitting or strolling, on the rocks and braes.

Then, having come back to the thoroughfares of traffic, and having satisfied the cravings of the inner man, one may as well, for all that is to be seen of other than recent origin and associations, take to the train, or to the bus along the wide and handsome main street of Newport, to Wormit and the south end of the Tay Bridge.

Here indeed is a modern marvel, comparable only, in our country, to the bridge across the Forth, on the other side of Fife. On a spur of rock, at the eastern corner of what had been a secluded little bay, was rivetted finally, in 1887, an enduring link of steel between North and South.

It was a triumph of engineering skill over the forces of nature; but it was a victory preceded by disaster. The First Tay Bridge, fully two miles in length, and formed of over eighty piers, supporting, in the central and deeper part of the river, girders of 245 feet span, was begun in 1871, and was finished seven years later. The construction was not unattended by warning; for in a violent gale in February 1877, when the bridge was approaching completion, two of the central girders were torn from their place, happily with no attendant loss of life. Eighteen months after the opening, the spirits of the air made another attempt to sweep this cobweb of man's making out of their customary path. On a wild night of tempest in the winter of 1879–80, on a Sunday, half-way between Christmas and the New Year, a terrific gust carried away the whole centre part of the fabric and flung it into the raging stream. A mail train from Edinburgh had just before entered upon the Bridge and it is supposed that its engine and six carriages, containing from seventy to eighty passengers, provided the purchase needed for the accomplishment of the work of destruction. All disappeared into the void amid flashes from the tortured metal, and there was none left to tell the tale.

A new Tay Bridge, with double rails and of greater strength, slightly greater in length and lower in height, sprang up before many years in the room of the old. It is placed some twenty yards farther upstream than its predecessor, whose abutments still show above water—for warning,

and for encouragement to persevere. With its
appearance, the Tay Ferries have been definitely
relegated into the background, although they
still serve important public purposes. The Tay
Bridge and its railways have, as one can see
with a glance of the eye, 'made' Newport, which
was inclined to drop into a backwater when the
line was first opened to Tayport; and it has
created Wormit. As one passes under an arch
of the Bridge that is built on dry land, a golf-
course opens on the left; villa houses are cropping up on the ridge above and pushing out
beyond the railway station, along the road that
leads, among other places, to Balmerino Abbey.
We prefer the lower and humbler footpath by
the shore. We are again out in the open, with
the breath of the sea in our nostrils, and away
from the works of man—this time with our faces
definitely set to the West.

Can that be called a shore path which, after
leaving behind the wreck of the old pier in
Wormit Bay, climbs up the side of grassy hills,
and if it climbs down into a deep dell—like that
at Kinburns—climbs out again to rise higher;
that keeps always between the wayfarer and
the Firth the thick coppice of blackthorn, hazel,
and taller trees that clothes the steep banks down
to high-water-mark? There are frequent peeps
down upon the sparkling waters, over which
shadows are drifting—reflections of the clouds
that are racing overhead before a brisk breeze—

and across to the northern end of the Bridge,
to the western suburbs of Dundee gathered
about Balgay Law, and to the Braes and the
Carse of Gowrie. But it would be ill work
seeking to follow closely the sea-margin at sea-
level, with choice often betwixt barnacled rock
and mudbank; and be sure the Monks of
Balmerino, when they wished to visit their
houses in Dundee, or their church and lands at
Barry, did not attempt it.

They would follow, and may have been the
first to form and use, the track we are retracing,
along what, in the old deeds, seems to have
been called 'Thorniebauk' and 'Scroggieside.'
And, besides, they had a ferry, and probably a
ferry-boat, of their own, for reaching the other
shore. At the end of the eighteenth century
the harbour of Balmerino was 'the chief place
on the south side of the Tay for shipping wheat
and barley for the Forth and Clyde Canal,' a
trade it took up when that for which it was first
designed, 'the shipping of lime from the Fife
hills to Dundee,' had failed. Balmerino was, in
fact, until the 'Balmerino Boat' sank one stormy
day fifty years ago in Dundee Harbour, and was
never replaced, one of the 'Ferries on Tay'—
perhaps the oldest of them all. Within living
memory passengers and goods continued to be
more or less regularly landed at the little pier,
and they are occasionally landed to this day,
when the haven looks more forlorn and deserted

than ever it has done since Queen Ermengarde
came hither to found the Abbey.

The Pease and the Scurr Hills on our left
were both of them original possessions of the
Monastery. They form part of the ramparts
raised by nature for the defence of Northern
Fife. Westward and southward these extend,
like some vast system of circumvallation, in
alternate ridge and valley, wall and ditch,
rising in Norman Law and Glenduckie to not
far short of the 1000-feet line. Passing the
limits of the Kingdom, they blend with the Ochil
range of which they are offshoots, and through
which there are road-passes only by Glenfarg,
the Path of Condie, and Gleneagles, until one
reaches Sheriffmuir and the 'battlefield of Scotland' around Stirling. To the east these coast
hills make their last heaves, in St Fort and
Scotscraig, before subsiding, in Tents Moor, to
the old sea-level.

Here, between Wormit and Balmerino, they
rise boldly and yet smoothly to three hundred
or four hundred feet; and here also have been
fights between Picts and Angles, and between
Scots and Danes, to say nothing of later com-
batants. A conflict, of which the name Battle
Law remains as witness, is said to have been
fought on the more inland height, looking down
on Bottomcraig and the road that passes the
present parish church and manse of Balmerino,
on its way to Abbey, Pier, and Kirkton. In

this valley, behind the Scurr Hill, are the woods
and the House of Naughton, said to have been
part of the guerdon of victory. Hays, successors
by marriage of the Lascelles, lived on Naughton
Craig for centuries, and are famous in Scottish
epic and legend. They were succeeded by
Morisons and Anstruthers, whose monuments,
with those of the Scrimgeour-Wedderburns of
Birkhill, are in the old Kirkton Graveyard; and
the ancient Castle of Naughton disappeared
with the building of the present mansionhouse.
Tradition affirms that Peasehills, or Peacehills,
got its name from the 'peace' patched up there
with the defeated invaders; and points to gold
coins, ornaments, and fragments of armour found
on the spot. But they were stronger in fighting and story-telling in the old times than in
philology; and even Fordun's explanation of
Balmerino as the 'Sailors' Town' is now thought
more plausible than accurate.

To resume, however, the pleasant footpath
way to this sequestered nook of Fife, you meet
with the choice of holding up towards the
scattered cottages of the Kirkton, or holding
forward past the Maw Craig and 'Samson's
Stone' to the mill and harbour at the mouth
of the burn. In neither case will you go wrong.
Up above there is a snug tea-room, as well as
a grand view. From the strand below is seen
one of the prettiest pictures of the Forth,
whether you look back, or forward, or across.

Lindores Abbey.

And here, as one may guess with confidence, was the landing-place of the Lady Ermengarde —second wife and widow of William the Lyon, daughter of the Earl of Beaumont, and great-granddaughter of the Conqueror, mother of Alexander II., and ancestress of the succeeding sovereigns of Scotland—when, out of gratitude for the health and the peace she had found at 'Balmurynach'—there is a choice of thirty-six ways of spelling the name—she resolved to plant there a house of Cistercian monks, dedicated to the Virgin and to her relative 'the most holy King Edward,' the Confessor.

This resolve, made sometime at the beginning of the second quarter of the thirteenth century, was promptly carried into execution, and on St Lucy's Day, 1229, a company of monks from Melrose, under Alan, their first Abbot, were able to enter and take possession. The Abbey was a monument of sacrifice, as well as of gratitude, for the foundress had first to purchase with a thousand marks the lands representing nearly the whole of the present parish, to which the Abernethies of Carpow had succeeded as Lay Abbots of the Culdee seat of Abernethy. It was built of a red stone from Nydie, beyond the Eden, where there is still quarrying. In its palmy days it must have been a goodly and beautiful habitation of peace, of a plan conforming to the Mother Church of Melrose, in having the cloister on the north side of the sanctuary and in other details. It was richly endowed with estates, fishings, benefices, rights, and privileges; and until near the time of its downfall was blessed in having no history to speak of, beyond the visits of royal and other guests, and the drowning of an early abbot who accompanied Sir Patrick Spens and the other 'good Scots lords' to Norway

Ermengarde and her son Alexander, another great benefactor, sojourned here repeatedly. They would ferry over from Dundee, or from Invergowrie, when coming from the royal palace at Forfar; for the Queen much affected the haunts, as well as the religious example, of her grandmother-in-law, the saintly Margaret.

In 1234 the body of the foundress, as says Wynton,

'With honure
Enteryd in halowd sepulture'

before the high altar of the Abbey Church. Like other landmarks of Balmerino, the grave will be looked for in vain. Of the Church itself there remains above ground only portions of the walls of the nave and north transept. Enough of the Chapter-House is left to show how goodly it was in ornament and proportions, although these have been mangled by later handling. What are taken to be penitential cells for refractory monks adjoin it; and exhibit a feudal frugality of light and space. There are fragments of the Sacristy and of the Abbots House, which, in Protestant

Chapter House, Balmerino Abbey.

times, became a manor-house for the Commendator and his successors. A relic of this period may be the carved armorial-stone, built into what was once the Abbey Barn, and now forming part of an adjoining farmsteading—the old 'Grange of Balmerino'—across the chevron bearings on which has been intruded the modern date '1849'!

What remains of Balmerino Abbey is kept in seemly order and condition. Although Daniel Defoe, who visited it in 1727, saw 'nothing worthy of observation, the very ruins being almost eaten up by time,' it is well deserving this reverent care, were it only for the ancient trees that are gathered around it. Chieftains among these are a magnificent old Spanish chestnut and a walnut of like or superior age. Beside them are set up two headless and limbless effigies. One of them is that of a knight, extracted from the wall of the Pier, which it had been thriftily used to repair; the other may be that of a monk, although lady visitors 'plump' for it being the effigy of a woman. Can it possibly be the maimed figure of Queen Ermengarde? Her stone coffin, containing her skeleton, is supposed to have been found, on the spot indicated by the records, by the tenant of the farm while, in the summer of 1831, he was engaged in 'carting away hewn stones from the piers and south wall of the church' to build a house in St Andrews. It was covered by a graveslab, which was 'broken in pieces,' while the bones found within were 'dispersed as curiosities through the country.'

The white freestone coffin itself was, it is said, 'broken down by the farmer's wife for sand to her kitchen floor.' To what base uses!

There are other carved stones built into the walls and houses of the hamlet; and further discoveries might be made by excavations of

Old Spanish Chestnut, Balmerino Abbey

foundations and clearing away rubbish heaps. The situation of the mill-pond in which the monks may have kept carp can easily be discerned in the hollow of the stream above the mill and bridge, and behind the ruins; but their chief supply of Lenten fare was doubtless drawn from their salmon and other fisheries in 'the salt-water Tay.' The 'Monks' Well' can still be pointed out, as can the 'Priors' Well,' and the 'Lady,' 'St John's,' 'Bride's,' and other springs in different parts of the parish; and the sites of 'Nut-yard' and 'Plum-yard,' of the 'Green,' the 'Butts,' and the 'Burnt Girnal' have been provisionally identified.

Who are responsible for the desolation that has overtaken this 'fair and noble structure'? The blame has been laid, perhaps too hastily, on the Lords of the Congregation, who, with Argyll and the Regent Moray at their head, and the 'reforming rabble' at their heels, came hither in the third week of June 1559, and set about 'casting down the monuments of idolatry.' But Admiral Wyndham and the English Fleet had been here twelve years before, and as the Abbey offered a stout resistance, by his own account he landed '300 men, with harque-bushes,' and 'bornt the Abbey with all thyngs that were in it, and certayn villages adjoining to yt with a great deal of corn.' And then account must be taken of the harryings of the monks themselves in a time of change, when 'Devil take the hindmost' was the motto of too many both of churchmen and laity in running away with the spoils; also of the wastage made by time and by modern vandalism.

Four centuries ago the glory of Balmerino was already beginning to wane. Yet the reputation for 'salubrity,' which first brought it into royal favour, has never failed. Ermengarde was not the only Queen who sought in it health and recruitment. Martine, the quaint seventeenth century chronicler of St Andrews, who was laird of Clairmont on the edge of Magus Moor, and secretary to Sharp, relates that Magdalen, the fragile consort of James V., 'being a tender Lady, the physician choosed this place (St Andrews), and the Abacie of Balmerinoch as having the best aers in the Kingdom for her residence and abode.' It is not proved, however, that she ever went there during her brief lease of life in Scotland; although Miss Strickland, from what scource of information is not known, states that 'she derived immediate benefit from the change of air; and perhaps if she could have been content to remain quietly there for a few weeks or months, equally good effects might have resulted to her as had formerly been the case with Queen Ermengarde. But as King James could not be with her in this monastic house, her desire for his society induced her to return to Holyrood, where she could enjoy his company.'

Mary Queen of Scots was certainly a visitor in January 1565, and probably lived in the Abbot's House, which was in existence till last century, as the guest of her Master of Requests, Sir John Hay, the first Lay Commendator of the Abbey. Later the lands were erected into

a barony, in favour of Sir James Elphinston of
Barnton, the first Lord Balmerino, who, after
having been sentenced to death, died quietly
at the Abbey of 'fever and waikness of the
stomach.' The more ill-fated Arthur, the sixth
Lord, who suffered on Tower Hill for his part
in the '45, is supposed to have lurked in some
cave or vault in the ruins, after his earlier
adventure in the '15, and before he escaped to
a vessel in the Firth of Tay, and to France.
The estates came into possession of the Earls
of Moray, descendants of the 'Good Regent'
and of the 'Bonnie Earl.'

Balmerino has a further and not so widely
appreciated claim to distinction as a place
of residence. It is best stated in the words
of the Rev. Andrew Thomson, the writer of
the description of the parish in the 'Old
Statistical Account'—himself a trophy of the
healthfulness of the parish in which he laboured
for fifty-four years and where he died when
over ninety. 'The wholesomeness of the
climate appears also in the fruitfulness of the
females. The present incumbent has often in
the course of ten years had an opportunity of
baptising twins; and there are two families in
the parish at present (1793), one of whom has
had thrice twins, and the other had five sons
at two births.' His son and successor, writer
of the article in the 'New Account' of forty
years later, caps the record by adding that

'this same individual, during his incumbency, baptised in the parish *three times trines.*'

Ministers' wives often retain a sprightly sense of humour, in spite of the wear and strain to which it is subjected by the multifarious congregational duties imposed upon this much-enduring class. To the ears of the mistresses of two adjacent manses, each of them a recent comer to North Fife, and each the mother of a rising young brood, the above interesting statistical facts were imparted in the course of conversation at two successive days' halting-places. Said one :

'Goodness preserve us! It's time I were out of Balmirnie!'

Said the other (addressing her husband), 'John! never accept a call from that parish!'

Five ministers of Balmerino since the Reformation, taking no account of such as have been 'translated' to wider spheres, have each laboured in their secluded parish for fifty years or more. One of them was that ardent presbyterian Walter Greig, who had a hand in the Metrical Version of the Psalms and in the Fife witch trials of the seventeenth century. It was in Mr Andrew Thomson's time that the parish church, dedicated to St Ayle, or Agilus, and situated 'within or near to the churchyard at Kirkton,' but apparently not intimately connected with the adjoining Abbey, moved to Bottomcraig, where it was a mile nearer the centre of population in Gauldry village across the hill ; for when the Mountain will not come to Mahomet, Mahomet must go to the Mountain.

A later veteran of the Church was the Rev. Dr James Campbell, a Crimean army chaplain, who wrote *Balmerino and its Abbey*, one of the earliest and best of parish histories, from which many of these notes have been borrowed. Remembrance of old intercourse and favours drew us back a mile to the Manse, built in the leafy shades where stood the manor-house of the Crichtons of Bottomcraig, and bearing testimony, in the glorious show of its rhododendrons and other plants, to the fertility of the soil, removed from the old Kirkton Manse, which had been used to fill up a gravel pit. As for the prospect from the 'Study Window,' which the present incumbent has brought within the vision of 'wireless' audiences, it fulfils the description of the historian of Balmerino of a site that 'commands a beautiful view of the Firth of Tay, the Carse of Gowrie, and the Sidlaw range of hills, with glimpses of the more remote Grampians, including Ben Voirlech on Loch Earn—a distance of about fifty miles in a straight line.'

It beckons us westward—on the road that leads to 'the confines of the Kingdom.'

THE CONFINES OF THE KINGDOM.

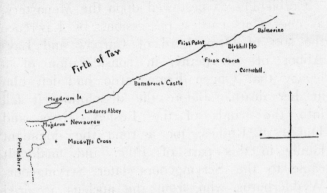

Lead on, Macduff !—*Macbeth* (amended).

IT is hardly practicable to keep to the coast-
line of the Firth on the way from Balmerino to its neighbour Abbey of Lindores,
and to the confines of the Kingdom of Fife
—at least in the first section of the tract,
which, for two or three miles, lies within the
grounds of Birkhill, formerly known as Corbiehill. The shore, west of the Pier, is seamed
by dens, covered with wood, mostly scrub oak,
and difficult of access, and, when reached, it
is difficult to traverse. It was part of the
'Wood of Balmerino,' which, under the monks,
had a Forester to look after it; and it is
thought that the site of his house may be
indicated by the ancient yews that, in double

251

line, form a hollow square near the House of Birkhill and cast an almost impenetrable shade that cannot have been often invaded since first they were planted.

Corbiehill was bestowed upon the Monastery, as one of its earliest possessions, by Lawrence the son of Orm, Lord of Carpow and Lay-Abbot of Abernethy, in consideration of a legacy that Queen Ermengarde had left him at her death. Before the dissolution, it fell into the hands of the Leslies, Earls and Dukes of Rothes, for a time the dominant family in this part of Fife; and finally it came to the Scrymgeours, later Scrymgeour-Wedderburns, who, from the nucleus acquired early in the eighteenth century at Wormit and the Wood of Balmerino, have become owners of a wide demesne, with Birkhill, over-looking the sea, as its stately manor-house. They claim derivation from those stout hench-men of Canmore and of Wallace who, from their forward valour in battle, were dubbed 'Skirmishers,' or, to be nearer the sound and sense, 'Scrimmagers'; and the head of the house is Hereditary Armour-bearer of Scotland and Constable of Dudhope, and is entitled to bear part of the Royal Arms, a Rampant Lion, wielding, 'for difference,' a scimitar, the heraldic substitute for the 'crooked sword,' with which in hand the ancestor of the race plunged into the Spey and won victory from the Men of Moray in one of their last rallies on behalf of the line of Macbeth. A rousing tale, if somewhat incoherent and contradictory as to dates and other details.

Who tries the route by the Birkhill Shore may find the barrier impassable beyond the salmon fishery pier at the Low Wood, unless he climbs down into, and out of, the Corbie Den, which means scrambling and sliding; and he is like to miss the ruins of the Chapel, in Flisk Wood, and in the parish of that name, where stone coffins have been found, and to which may belong a fragment, unearthed at Birkhill, of a cross of Celtic type, with an archaic representation of the Crucifixion. Down the steep, braken-clad slope leads a footpath to the Flisk Shore; and here, at all states of the tide, one must pick a way for a mile or two over rough shingle and pebbles, between rock and scrub-wood and muddy sea margin, to Flisk Point, and to Flisk Kirk and Manse. The mats of decomposed peat that strew the foreshore yield no relief to the feet, for they turn to slush under the tread. They are doubtless frayed ends of the submarine forest and peat-moss which, geologists tell us, lines this coast for several miles.

It is half ebb, and blowing half a gale from the west; and a powerful current crested with foam is rushing between us and the sand and mud-flats that are emerging out of the middle

Firth. At all times except high water, the Earn and the Tay retain in the upper part of the Firth something of their identity and of their colour in the South and North Deeps ; but the stream that flows past Comrie and that which runs by Dunkeld and under Perth bridge are united in this broad current that comes surging round Flisk Point and its fishers' bothy. A perilous voyage, surely, is our thought as we watch the two fishermen haul up their coble and shoulder their 'graith'; and, entering into conversation with them, we learn that they have come eleven miles, through wild weather and over wild water, all the way from Kinfauns, on the farther side of Tay, where, from of old, the Abbey owned 'Stok and Garth' fishings.

To the needless question, 'Are you wet?' came the sarcastic reply, 'Only frae the airm-pits doun.'

The 'red fish'—salmon and grilse—were greatly relished at the tables of the monks of Lindores and Balmerino ; and the fishing industry, which included the capture of sperling, or smelts, and occasionally of the seal, was of even more importance than now on these shores, down to the date, more than a hundred years ago, when stake-net fishing was forbidden by law. But the fishermen of the Tay if a scantier, are still a hardy and courageous race.

A pebble, as big as a house, is said to lie near the Point, flung across from the Sidlaws by the Giant Macbeth. We do not stop to discover it, but climb up through the wooded den to the lonely Kirk of this seaside parish. There is apparently no one within sight or hearing. Yet Flisk Manse has harboured notable men; and in the centre of the little kirkyard lie Andrew Leslie, fifth Earl of Rothes, and others of his name and kin.

Flisk retained its rectorage teinds, and was under the lay patronage of the House of Leslie; it was a prize worth having for Church pluralists. Its rector in 1527 was rector also of St Andrews University; and in that year he was one of the judges who tried and condemned to the stake Patrick Hamilton. Sir James Balfour was parson of Flisk at the time of the Reformation; he had been Knox's companion in the galleys but afterwards came, with other scions of the Balfours of Mountquhannie, under his greater commination as 'blasphemous Balfour'; while Dr Robertson stigmatises him as 'the most corrupt man of his age'—a strong phrase. He is suspected of having had a hand in Rizzio's slaughter; it was in his brother's house, at Kirk-o'-Field, that Darnley was slain; but all this did not prevent him from being the learned author of that legal classic *Balfour's Praticks*, and rising to be President of the Court of Session. Another minister of Flisk, John Wemyss, became Principal of St Leonard's College, St Andrews, before the century was out ; and a later incumbent was Dr John Fleming, Professor of Natural Philosophy in Aberdeen.

Ballanbreich, or Bambreich as it is familiarly called, stands full in sight a couple of miles

Ballanbreich Castle.

farther along the coast, at the corner of a little wood, and near the sea. The great grey castle of the Leslies has long been a roofless ruin. It has been stripped of its adornments, except some remains of corbelling, arcading, and battlements, and bears no armorials, date, or other inscription. Though many of its facing-stones have been carried away for utilitarian purposes, it is a grand fabric of hewn ashlar-work, built

F.F.

Macduff's Cross.

mainly, like Lindores Abbey, of the red stone
of Black Earnside, large in design and commanding in situation. Its builders, the Earls
of Rothes, inherited the lands in the Bruce's
time, through marriage with an heiress of the
Abernethies, and it was for centuries the chief
seat of their authority as Hereditary Sheriffs
of Fife, before they moved to Leslie, and the
estate passed on to the Dundases of Zetland.

When George, the first Earl of Rothes, had
his possessions in Fife, Perth, Aberdeen, and
Moray formed, in 1458, into a single Barony,
it was called after this stronghold on the Tay ;
and when the seventh Earl, John, who carried
the sword at the coronation of Charles II. at
Scone, was, in 1680, made Duke of Rothes,
he chose as his second title that of Marquis
of Ballanbreich. Many notable things have
happened at this lordly Castle by the Sea. From
it Norman Leslie, Master of Rothes, who held
a charter of Ballanbreich, must have ridden in
gloomy mood on the direful business of the
' slaughter of the Cardinal,' to be joined, perhaps,
on the road to St Andrews by his brother William
and his truculent uncle, John Leslie, of Parkhill, both of them deeply implicated in the
crime. Mary, on that journey through Fife in
1565, when she was so 'magificently banquetted,
that partridges sold for a crown apiece,' stayed
for a night or two at Ballanbreich, and, among
other transactions, nominated another John

Leslie, afterwards Abbot of Lindores and Bishop of Ross, and her faithful friend and ambassador in exile, to be a Lord of Session and a Canon of Moray.

Now there is not even a footpath to the spot where it hides among the planes and oaks on the brink of a bank washed by the waters of the Firth, almost abreast of the houses and parks of Errol, on the opposing shore. No traces are left around it of its swan and fish ponds and orchards and the other marks of wealth and luxury it boasted when, under the magnificent Duke, the sober Covenanters of Fife were scandalised by the 'sports' played on the Sabbath day in its courtyard. Of its chapel hard by no stone is left on another, nor is a chestnut-tree left from its great avenue; the glory has clean departed from Ballanbreich.

At Flisk Kirk and at Ballanbriech Castle, one is only a few hundred yards from the highway from Newport to Newburgh, by which, it need scarcely be said, there is much easier and quicker access to these remote parts of Fife than by scrambling along a pathless beach.

Leaving, as fit only for a mood of adventurous trespassing, the shore line from Balmerino to Newburgh, we follow, on a subsequent visit, the public road between these points. It is a road of ups and downs, that dives down a brae in sight of the bluffs of the Black and Green

Craigs, to rise again as it skirts the flanks of the Fliskmill and Logie Hills, and to curve, along the sides of Braeside—by 'Wallace's Bridge' and 'Wallace's Camp,' the site of that hero's victory, in 1300, over his English foes at Black Earnside—before descending upon the Abbey of Lindores and its 'New burgh. For here the hills of Northern Fife again press near to the salt water, leaving only a narrow selvage of ploughed land, an obvious gate of entrance and of defence, between slope and shore.

From Balmerino you can reach this old main line of communication between St Andrews and Lindores by either the north or the south side of Coultra Hill and Green Hill, rising, both of them, to six hundred feet, covered with wood and crowned, the one by the 'Gallowstone,' which Dr Campbell regards as the remains of an ancient dolmen beside which justice was administered by the Bailie of the Abbot of Balmerino, and the other by a cairn and cist. By the first way you come to Demonds and Thornton and the woods that surround the home farm of Birkhill. The more southern road, by the Prior's Well and the hamlet of Coultra, must have been familiar to the fathers of the Cistercian House on their way to their dependant Preceptory of Gadvan, in the neighbouring parish of Dunbog, and to their rich lands in the upper part of the Howe of Fife. The boundary of another hill parish, that of

Creich, is crossed at Corbiehill before Flisk is entered, and Dunbog actually sends a strip— the 'Highham Plouts'—a thread of the Fringe —down to the edge of the Firth, between Flisk and Abdie.

Coultra—the 'Hill of the Hazels'—is an offshoot of the range which reaches its highest point in Norman's Law—once Dunmore, the 'Great Fort'—and that sends up its sharpest salient farther west in the Clatchart Craig. These North Fife hills leading us towards the Perth border and the former seats of authority in Southern Pictland, at Abernethy and at Forteviot, are intriguing in their names; and if you care, as we do, to make the stiff ascent of Fliskmill Hill by the side road that leads to Luthrie station you will have rich reward. For, below the hills that encircle the cup in which lies the old Castle and Church of Creich and the cottages of Brunton—a hamlet of 'bonnet lairds'—there is spread at your feet the whole history of the country.

'Fliskmill,' more correctly 'Fliskmullan,' never had a mill; but the name described accurately the round, bald ridge, now pine-covered, which forms a buttress to the cairn-topped peak of Norman's Law behind it. But what is one to make of Lyndemus, and Pittachop, and Whirly Kip; of Craigsimmie, and Craiglug, and Drumnod; or, farther away, of Lumbenny and Lumquhat, Skirlbare and Craigsparrow? Was the name-

father of 'Jock's Hole,' on the Balmerino
Shore, identical with that of 'Jock's Lodge,'
on the Abdie Shore? The Balmerino scribes
must have had difficulty in interpreting names
like 'Craigengrugiesfauld,' and 'Cleikamscleuch,'
and 'Duchrone'; or at least, as with that of
the Abbey itself, they spelt them in a great
variety of ways. Even the sandbanks and
shore rocks of the Tay have a suggestive
or puzzling nomenclature — 'Sure - as - Death,'
'Eppie's Taes,' 'Durward's Scalp,' and, farther
east, 'Pluck-the-Craw.'

Every name in and behind these hills has
its own tale and its own atmosphere. Rathillet,
for instance, brings up the fateful figure of
Hackston, sitting dourly on his horse, on
Magus Moor, while Archbishop Sharp was
being slain—a consenter to the deed, though
refusing to actually embrue his hands in blood.

Many noble, and many ugly things in history
and literature have been hatched to birth
below or in sight of Norman's Law. The
Mount of Sir David Lyndesay, the first of
the ten 'Lord Lyons' that sprang from this
side of Fife, is not far away on the farther
slope of Lindiferronhill, far seen and easily
marked by the 'Hopetoun Monument' on its
crest. Myrecairnie and Murdochcairnie are
names that suggest tragedy—

> Seek yonder brake beneath the cliff;
> There lies Red Murdoch, stark and stiff.

Accordingly, we hear of young Ayton of Inch-
dairnie, on the way to visit his kin at Murdochcairnie, shot by Royalist dragoons. It was on
the road past it to Cupar, also, that Crichton
of Bottomcraig, in 1619, encountered his enemy,
Fyfe of Kirkton, who ran him through the body,
and rode away and was never heard of again.
Murdoch, Duke of Albany, was owner of much
land, the inheritance of the old Thanes of Fife,
in this region before his forfeiture and execution in the time of James I. of Scots. His
name is attached to the parish of Logie-
Murdoch and to other places.

Over the hills, also, and not far away, are
Melville and Halhill of the Melvilles, Parbroath
of the Setons, Collairnie of the Barclays, Colluthie
of the Carnegies, Lordscairnie of the 'Tiger Earl'
of Crawford. Luthrie, in Creich, is thought to
have been the birthplace of Alexander Henderson, who at least 'mortified' two thousand
marks, 'for the encouragement of a school-
master' in the parish; and in the centre—such
as it is—of industry and population in Creich
was born, also, that worthy member of a later
episcopate, Bishop Sage. To the Beatons of
Creich attaches romance as well as history.
In the ruined Castle was born Dame Janet
Beaton, that 'Lady of Branksome,'

Of Bethune's line of Picardie,

who figures in the 'Lay of the Last Minstrel.'

Her niece—also born at Creich of the same blood as the Archbishop and the Cardinal of the name—was Mary Beaton, of the 'Queen's Maries.'

These ladies, according to the gossipy John Martin, appear to have derived their beauty from the mother of the one and grandmother of the other, Janet Hay, daughter of a Provost of Dundee. 'It has been observed and reported,' he says, 'that the race and people of the Beatons of Balfour were always black and not beautiful and fair. But ever after the Laird of Creich (Sir John Beaton) married this Janet, the Beatons of Creich have ever been yellow-haired for the most part, and of beautiful countenances.'

Whether you descend upon it from the hillside, where the 'Black Wood of Ironside,' on which the Scottish Champion rallied his men, casts scarcely a patch of shadow, or whether you find your way up to it from the Waterside and the 'Pow,' where only at low water, and with the aid of faith, can you make out the stones of the pier on which the monks landed their salmon or set out to visit their subject church of Dundee, you come rather unexpectedly upon the Abbey of Lindores. If you approach from the west and from the side of Newburgh, it is like that you may miss it altogether, drawn astray, when within a gunshot of the Abbey Gateway, by a signboard that directs you a couple of miles into the interior—

to 'Lindores,' the village and the loch of the name, by a road that leads under the great Clatchard Craig and the Mare's Craig, both of them in course of being quarried away, and past the old Castle of Denmyln and the 'cottages of Glenburnie.'

What was once a wealthy Abbey, older and more famous than Balmerino, has become an inconspicuous group of red and grey walls, surrounded and invaded by trees. Lindores has not merely been shorn of its beauty; it has been scalped and flayed. Instead of being, like the other House of the Old Religion, trimly kept in its age and decay, it is left to moulder in a disorder that is not to be admired.

The gate is padlocked, and we wander around the walls seeking for an entrance. Great fragments of masonry lean up, as if for support, against ancient trees that scarcely seem younger; with this aid we look over into the enclosure, and discover a big black Angus bull roaming loose within the cloister. Not an enticing sight for such as would sit down quietly to sketch and to meditate!

The custodier, who is also in charge of the dairy-farm of Parkhill, in which the ruins are incorporated, comes to our relief, and is kindly and communicative. We remark upon the strange guardian of a historic site, as, at the opening of the gate, the bull comes forward to meet us. 'Ay, he's a fine billie yon—a grand watchdog.

The folk that come in wi' an ill-will gang oot wi'
a het fit.'

And there is no more to be said.

It is difficult in the confusion of walls and
accumulation of rubbish of what is still a 'wilder-
ness' to trace the original plan of the buildings,
Early Pointed in style, of which more survives
than first appears—to make out the position of
the western tower ; the south wall of the aisleless
nave ; the presbytery ; the south and part of the
north transept ; the chapter-house and sacristy ;
the fratery and the walls surrounding the cloister
garth. Those opening from the east side of
the cloister, especially the vaulting of the slype
or sacristy, are in the best state of preservation
—which is not saying much. The lower part
of the effigy of a priest—probably an abbot—
leans against the wall along with other sepulchral
fragments and ornaments. None of them can
be identified with David, Duke of Rothesay, the
ill-fated heir to the throne, who was hastily
buried here in 1401 after having been done to
death in Falkland Palace by myrmidons of the
Duke of Albany, as related in *The Fair Maid
of Perth*. Miracles were wrought at the spot
until, says Boece, 'King James the First began
to punis his slayaris, and fra' that time furth the
miraclis ceissit.'

The spirit of Sir Walter Scott haunts these
cloistral shades ; another and for years a living
occupant of the Abbey was James, the ninth

and last of the line of the 'Black Douglases'—
'Greystiel' of *The Lady of the Lake*—who
sought and found retirement here as an alternative to death : 'He that can no better must e'en
be a monk.'

David, Earl of Huntingdon, Scott's 'Knight
of the Leopard,' was founder of this Benedictine
House of the Tyronesian Order, which was
colonised by monks from Kelso at the end of
the twelfth century and dedicated to St Mary
and St Andrew in gratitude for 'the taking of
Ptolemais in Palestine,' or, according to another
account, for the rescue from drowning of the
wandering hero of *The Talisman*—during a
storm in the Firth of Tay. Other visitors were
his brother, William the Lyon ; the Second and
the Third Alexanders, one of whom brought
interdict on Lindores and Scotland through his
quarrel with the Pope, while the other had his
young son and heir buried here. Edward I.,
the 'Hammer of the Scots,' was here in 1291
and again in 1296 (this time on his way from
Perth to St Andrews, with probably the 'Stone
of Destiny,' filched from Scone, among his
baggage). Between these visits came that *Roy
Faineant*, John Baliol, and later Lindores saw
David II., that unworthy Bruce, and sundry
Stuart sovereigns, including, of course, Mary.

Before her visit, an angry Dundee mob had,
in 1543, assailed the Abbey, 'ejecting the monks
and destroying the furnishings and ornaments.'

Then fell the storm of the Knox Reformation; but worse misfortune and degradation may have come upon Lindores Abbey later, when it was in the hands of greedy Lay Commendators, and when neighbouring farmers and townsfolk made the buildings a quarry from which they drew stones to erect walls and houses. The lands were erected into a barony conferred on Patrick Leslie of Pitcairlie, from whom sprang David Leslie, Lord Newark, the victor of Philiphaugh; and they came later to the Dundases.

The most famous of the Abbots was that great theologian and inquisitor Lawrence, the founder, or at any rate one of the founders, of St Andrews University, who helped to burn the Lollardists, Resby and Crawar. Perhaps the most momentous event it has witnessed was the meeting here in 1306 of three puissant knights, Sir Gilbert Hay of Errol, Sir Neil Campbell of Lochaw, and Sir Alexander Seton, and the sealing before the high altar of the vow they had made to 'defend the King Robert the Bruce and hes crowne to the last of their blood and fortunes.' It was the refounding of Scottish independence on a surer basis than that attempted by Wallace when he stole hither out of Black Earnside Wood for water for his wounded men—was it from the 'Monk's Well,' or the 'Abbot's Well'?—and as Blind Harry relates:

> Drank himselff, syne said, with sobyr mood,
> The wyn of Frans methocht nocht halff so good.

The Champion is not forgotten in Newburgh tradition, and the Clatchard Craig, which faces the Abbey with a sheer cliff of two hundred feet, is pointed to as the stone whereon he whetted his great two-handed sword!

'Kings, warriors, statesmen who have borne a considerable part in history have trod,' says Dr Laing, the historian of Lindores, 'the courts of the Abbey. These are deserted and ruined; but the place where brave men have walked, where brave words have been spoken, and where for centuries men worshipped and praised God can never become, in the eyes of the thoughtful, mere common ground.' We were thoughtful, as we left Lindores; leaving the bull—and the pigeons, crows, and jackdaws—in possession. As we passed through the gate, a crow emerged from the ivy with a pigeon's egg in its bill—an analogue of the fate of Lindores!

The buildings extended beyond the present bounds. In the field across the road there are considerable masses of the high and well-built walls that enclosed the orchards and other adjuncts of the monastery. Sculptured frag·ments have been built into the dwelling-house, at the Abbey, where one of the old yews had just been cut down to give light to a kitchen, and where, through a window, we could see the floor of a room strewn with apples, but none of the fruit of those 'vastly big old

pear-trees,' for which, according to Sir Robert
Sibbald and others, Lindores was celebrated.
It is 'a right sweet situation, a most rich soil'

Farm House, Lindores Abbey.

—brought specially from Ireland as is said; and
the pear-trees, or their descendants, may still be
blossoming and bearing fruit in the orchard, as

in the famous fruit gardens of the neighbouring burgh. But it is a right sad end to an
auld sang.

It is but a spang from the Abbey to its once
dependant vill of Newburgh-on-Tay, and, after
pacing the good half-mile of the street of the
little town, it is only another and longer spang
from Newburgh out of Fife. We are come,
when Mugdrum is overpassed, to 'the end of
the Kingdom,' which is thought to have had
the name bestowed on it on account of things
done, or spoken, in this corner of it, fuller
than any other of fateful happenings and
Delphic utterances. Newburgh was 'Novus
burgus juxta Monasterium de Lindoris,' when
it was made a burgh of barony, subject to
the Abbot and convent by Alexander III. in
1266, and, even then, it is claimed, it was
only new by comparison. It became a royal
burgh in 1457, confirmed in 1631; but neither
then nor at any subsequent date did Newburgh
send a representative of its own to the Scots
parliament.

Newburgh has always found sufficient interest
and occupation in its own affairs and in that of
the neighbourhood. It looks clean, well-built,
and prosperous enough; but not exceptionally
lively. Nor is the idea dispelled that it takes
life and business easily when one danders down
to the Shore and Pier; there is not the 'stir'
there that we are told was seen when vessels

were in the habit of unloading in order that
their cargoes might be transhipped to craft of
lighter draft for conveyance to Perth, and when

Old Houses, Newburgh.

large quantities of salmon and grilse were
being boiled for transport to the Continental
markets.

A big linoleum factory has settled on the
Shore and gives the place employment. But
salmon-fisher cobles plying their craft between

us and the fields and reedbeds of Mugdrum island, a fleet of wild swans and cygnets
paddling downstream past the pierhead, and
flights of gulls fluttering around it are the chief
signs of life and movement about the harbour.

Becket's Close, Newburgh.

The days are legendary when 'Newburgh
supplied the navy of Great Britain with steady,
well-behaved, and gallant mariners.' At one
time it gave its mind to husbandry, and later

to hand-loom weaving; it has now a variety of occupations, of which, if linoleum is the chief, the housing of summer visitors is not the least. It may not be so well provided, in number at least, with licensed houses, as at the date of the 'New Statistical Account,' when there were '25 in the Burgh, 4 at the Shore, and 2 in the parish outside.' Amenities are not neglected, as the trees in the High Street, of which the handsome spire of the Town House is one of the ornaments, declare; yet the old is not despised, and there are thatched roofs, and forestairs, and inscribed doorways for those who choose to look for them.

Newburgh parish was disjoined in 1622 from Abdie, which hems it in against the Perthshire frontier and cuts it in parts. The suburb—not misnamed—of Mount Pleasant, which hangs above the town from the steep slopes of the White Craig, is in Abdie parish, whose name is supposed to indicate a Culdee foundation, earlier than, and ousted by, Lindores. At all events, old Abdie Church, the three-light window of whose ruined gable hangs over the lovely Loch of Lindores, claims to be the senior of the Tyronesian Abbey. The 'Lecturer's Inch,' and the fragments of the Castle within the grounds of the modern Inchrye Abbey, are among the evidences of ancient occupation and sanctity. The later Castle of Denmyln, now a group of bare walls among gardens and cottages by the

18

road leading down to Lindores Abbey and the burgh, was one of the ancestral homes of Sir James Balfour, the annalist and herald—Lord

Denmyln Castle, Newburgh.

Lyon in the reign of Charles I. and II.—whose grave is in Abdie Kirk.

A monument of far earlier date and more curious interest is hidden within the grounds of Mugdrum House, reached by traversing the whole length of the Newburgh High Street, to the gates beside the War Memorial, the bowling green, and the railway station. It is not the crumbling remains of the former mansion of the Hays of Leys and Mugdrum, for

hat dates no farther back than the eighteenth
century. Easily missed, although set on a
ridge close to the bounds of Fife and Perth,
and commanding a grand view of the meeting
of the streams of the Earn and Tay, with
vistas of the valleys and hills to which they
lead, looking directly down on the Firth, now
narrowed and divided by the mile-long island
of Mugdrum and across to Kinnoull and the
Sidlaws, is Mugdrum Cross.

It has strangely escaped the attention it
deserves from its situation and its character—
in part, perhaps, because it is closely invested
by trees in an obscure corner of Fife, and also
doubtless because the interest and speculations
of the curious have been diverted to its rival,
'Cross Macduff,' only a mile or so away, Yet,
to look at, this is much the more imposing and
enigmatical relic of the 'dark ages' of Scotland
and of Fife. It is a monolith rising some twelve
feet above its socket—more if the fragment
lying at its foot is to be taken as part of the
original stone—and inscribed on the side turned
to the east (the other side is so weathered as
to be undecipherable) with the figures, half-
effaced, of hunters on horseback, engaged, if
one may judge by the lively scene on one of
the bottom panels, in the chase of the wild
boar. An art not despicable is shown in the
moulding of the animals and in the much worn
Celtic ornamentation on the edges of the stone.

Mugdrum Cross.

It was intended, we may well believe, to record the fame or piety of some Pictish chief or saint—to point a moral and adorn a tale. But time and the winds that blow past it from the Highlands and the North Sea have robbed it of its message and its meaning.

The saint, as has been conjectured, may be St Adrian, whose Chapel and Coffin are at the Pilgrim's Haven on the May, and who seems to have been much honoured in this part of Fife, where the Churches of Flisk and Abdie were dedicated to him, and where he is mysteriously associated with 'Cross Macduff' itself. The name Adrian may be a form of that of the Celtic Saint Odhrain. It has in an ignorant later time undergone strange changes. Magidrin, or Macgridin, is the local form, which has been corrupted to 'Mugdrum,' and debased a stage farther to 'St Muggin's Seat' on the top of one of the Creich hills. Most singular of all is the change to 'Exmagirdle'—'Ecclesia Ma Odhrain'—in the parish of Dron, to which an ancient causeway is said to have run seven miles from Newburgh-on-Tay. It is of the lasses of this village on the more sunless slope of the Ochils that the rhyme runs:

> The lasses o' Exmagirdle
> They may weel be dun,
> For from Martinmas to Whitsunday
> They never see the sun.

But it is time we were setting forth for

Macduff's Cross, and for final parting from the Fringes of Fife.

A mile of air separates the two Crosses, but it is two strenuous miles by the road, up which we toil in the teeth of more than half a gale of westerly wind, over the shoulder of Ormiston Hill, which may take its name from Orm, the father of Lawrence of Carpow—lying in the haugh below us, but across the Perth border— once lord of these parts. As we mounted breathlessly upwards to greater heights of the Newburgh Common it was easy to fall into the mood of the redhanded homicide fleeing to the refuge of the Cross with the avenger of blood close on his heels.

Glad would we have been to have complied with the first part of the prescribed ritual, and to have drank and washed hands in one, if not in all, of the 'Nine Wells.' But the cold, clear springs have been tapped and gathered into a cistern-house; and one has to mount, with the old hill road to Auchtermuchty, almost to the watershed, and quite to the limits of Fife before the pedestal of 'Cross Macduff' looms up in a grass field with cattle grazing peacefully around it. Only the pedestal is left, and as there is no mark of a socket, men, becoming too sceptical, as they were at one time too credulous, concerning this relic of antiquity have been led to question whether there has ever been a cross, or at least a cross of stone or if its purpose had ever been more than that of a boundary, or at most a girth or sanctuary, mark.

This, however, would be to make away with one of the oldest and most persistent and circumstantial of Fife traditions. Every one has heard the story of how the Thane of Fife in Malcolm Canmore's time asked for and obtained from that monarch three gifts, as recompense for the services he had rendered. Macduff was not particularly modest in his requests which, according to Buchanan, were, first 'that his posterity should place the King who was to be crowned in the Chair of State; second, that they should lead the van of the King's armies; and third, that if any of his family were guilty of unpremeditated slaughter, he should pay a fine,' regulated by the rank of the victim. As elaborated by other writers, the third of these 'privileges of Clan Macduff,' the last to claim which is said to have been a Spence of Wormiston, in the sixteenth century, was subject to the conditions that not only should he wash away the bloodstains nine times in the Nine Wells, and fasten the fine—nine cows, with a 'colpendach,' or yearling heifer, and proportionately less if the slain was only a woman or a child—to the nine rings in the stone, but give evidence that he was within nine degrees of kin to the Thane of Fife, and that he had committed the deed in 'suddand

chaudmelle,' or without premeditation, failing
which he might be put to death on the spot
and his grave added to the cairns that were
grouped around the Cross until they were wiped
away by the thrifty hands of modern agriculture.

No wonder that this was accounted an
uncanny place—a tryst for the 'witch covins,'
and to be avoided after nightfall by godfearing
people. Only a hundred yards away was
'Sir Robert's Prap,' marking the spot where
a Balfour of Denmyln was slain in duel with
a Makgill of Rankeilour. All the details of the
legend run, it will be seen, in threes, or multiples
of three. No doubt there is a mystic meaning
somewhere. A substratum of real history is
below the amplifications, if one could but remove
from it the later growth of myth. The holes
in the pedestal have been pronounced to be
enlarged cupmarks, which only give 'Cross
Macduff' a much older pedigree. The Reformers,
on the march from Perth, are said to have
overthrown the shaft and broken it in pieces—
it has even been said to have been built into
a house in Newburgh. But was there a shaft?
And was there ever an inscription? The learned
Sir John Skene—a Fife laird of the sixteenth
century—says that he was able to read 'sundry
barbarous words and verses.' Sir James Balfour,
who lived close by the Cross, found only some
dispersed and outworn characters, Roman and
Saxon. Sir Robert Sibbald, also a Fifer by

descent, could read nothing on the pedestal
and see nothing of the shaft. What has been
handed down, in sundry versions, reads like
gibberish, of which these lines come nearest
to being intelligible :

> Propter Macgidrum, et hoc oblatum accipe semel
> Hæredum, super lymphato lapide labem ;

which, in Sibbald, is thus roughly paraphrased :

> For Saint Mackgidder's sake, and this oblation,
>   And by their only washing at this stone,
> Purg'd is the blood shed by that generation,
>   This privilege pertains to them alone.

Much better give up the conundrum than
puzzle over a mystery of so many centuries'
standing. More worth remembering are Scott's
lines. One cannot well come and look abroad
from this mountain edge of Fife without repeat-
ing them :

> Mark that fragment,
> I mean that rough-hewn block of massive stone,
> Placed on the summit of this mountain pass,
> Commanding prospect wide o'er field and fell,
> And peopled village and extended moorland,
> And the wide ocean and majestic Tay,
> To the far distant Grampians.

> 'Twas the pedestal
> On which in ancient times a cross was reared,
> Carved with words which foil philologists ;
> And the events it did commemorate
> Were dark, remote, and undistinguishable
> As were the mystic characters it bore.

Like a spectre charged with messages of welcome and of warning, the portentous figure of Macduff has stalked beside us round the whole of these Fringes of Fife. He met us almost as soon as we set foot across the threshold of his ancient domain—on the ridge of Bordie and under the towers of Dunimarle. From point to point we have fallen under his shadow, or the shadow of one of the many Castles of the Thane of Fife; and the very winds and waves have seemed to

> Bring us word Macduff has fled

from his pursuers, across some sombre heath or stormy arm of the sea; but fled only to return again, defiant and victorious. And here, on the very confines of the Kingdom, and after a long lapse of years, he stands to bid us farewell, the favourite of fortune, the arrester of fate, the man to whose word revenge and justice, the law and the law's penalties, have to bow.

By 'Macduff's Cross,' that place of meeting between hoary tradition and authentic, but scarcely less mysterious and blood-stained, history, he seems to point backwards to scenes that are woven into the destinies of Scotland; and at the same time to beckon us onward to still wider horizons and higher achievement. At the ferry of Kincardine-on-Forth, the third part of a century ago, we gazed behind us up the great hollow of Central Scotland towards

Stirling Castle and the Abbey Craig, and, shining in the morning light, those fair and famous plains under the bluffs of the Ochils and the Campsie heights, and beyond these

From the Forth Bridge, looking west.

and for background, towards the mountains that gather around the sources of the Forth and the basin of Loch Lomond.

Here, on a bare hillside overlooking the point where the second great inlet from the North Sea merges in the fresh water drawn from the Grampians—here, with Mugdrum Inch and the richest part of Gowrie and Strathearn at our feet, with King's Seat and Dunsinane, Kinnoull and Moncrieffe standing over against us like sentinels, and with Abernethy and Forteviot hiding round the shoulder of Pitcairlie Hill, we gaze through not one, but two great avenues leading into the heart of the Highlands—the way to Perth and Scone, to Glamis and Forfar, to Dunkeld and Killicrankie, and to 'Rannoch and the Isles'; the way, also, to Dupplin and Crieff, to Comrie and Balquhidder; in witness whereof, the giants of Drumalban—Schiehallion and Ben Lawers, Ben More and Ben Vorlich—lift up their spears into the sunset.

INDEX

Edinburgh : Printed by W. & R. Chambers, Limited.

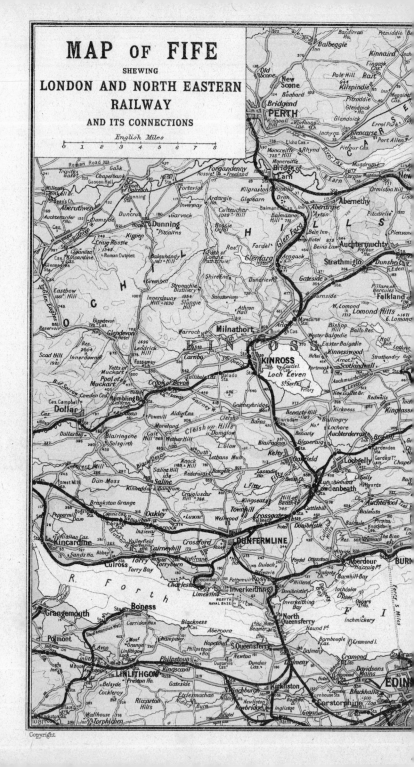

MAP OF FIFE

SHEWING

LONDON AND NORTH EASTERN
RAILWAY

AND ITS CONNECTIONS

English Miles

0 1 2 3 4 5 6 7 8

Copyright.

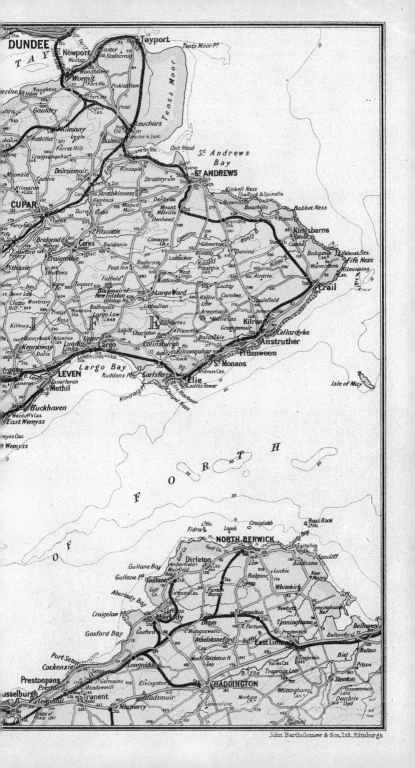

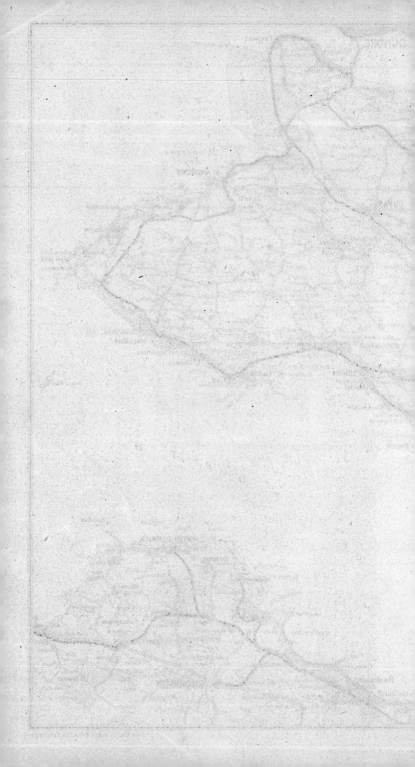